Fishing
Oneida Lake

Fishing Oneida Lake

SPIDER RYBAAK

Burford Books

Photos on pages 14, 26, and 40 by Susan Douglass.

Printed in the United States of America

10 9 8 7 6 5 4 3 2 1

Library of Congress Cataloging-in-Publication Data
Rybaak, Spider.
    Fishing Oneida Lake / Spider Rybaak.
        pages cm
    1. Fishing—New York (State)—Oneida Lake.   2. Bass fishing—New York (State)—Oneida Lake.   3. Ice fishing—New York (State)—Oneida Lake.
I. Title.
    SH529.R93 2015
    799.17'730974762—dc23   2014040193

**To Susan,
the best catch of all**

CONTENTS

SPRING

SUMMER

AUTUMN

WINTER

ACKNOWLEDGMENTS

WRITING A BOOK of this scope by myself would've been torturous, dragging me away for unbearable periods of time from really important stuff like Susan, the cats, and my favorite fishing holes. Numerous people helped me with everything from revealing secret hotspots and fishing techniques to telling me about the lake's dynamics, traditions, and personalities. I don't always carry a notepad so I don't have all the names, but here's a list of those I remember: Andrew Benbenek, Gene Carey, Ray Chittenden, Wes Coy, Al Daher, James Daher, Jerry Donahue, Robert Donahue, Susan Douglass, Bill Evans, Jim Everard, Gary Fischer, Frank Flack, Dave France, Todd Frank, Kim Goffredo, Rob Goffredo, John Hrynyk, Walter Hrynyk, Randy Jackson, J. Michael Kelly, Joe Lampreda, Lindsay Lampreda, Jake Maxwell, Mike McGrath, Burt Menninger, Rick Miick, Larry Muroski, Jim Novak, Stan Ouellette, Scott Prindle, Capt. Carl Rathje, Pete Rich, Pete Rowell, John Rucando, Dr. Lars G. Rudstam, Lorne Rudy, Staash Rybaak (Cousin Staash), Chris Scriba, Don Sheldon and Scott VanDerWater.

MAPS OF ONEIDA LAKE

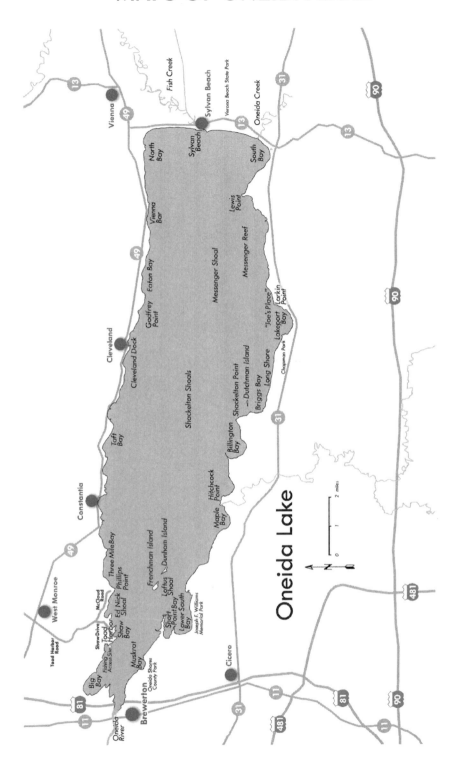

Oneida Lake

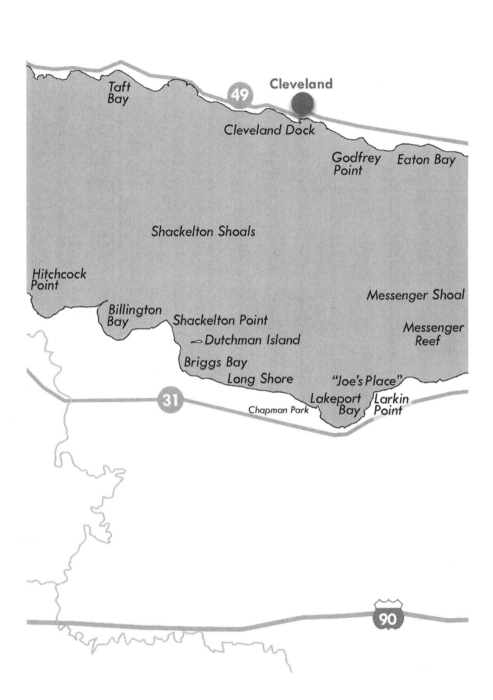

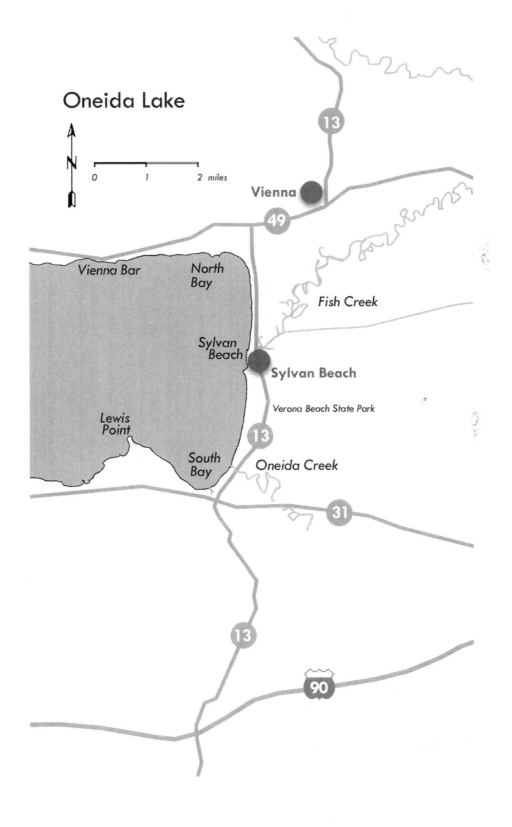

Oneida Lake

N

0   1   2 miles

13

Vienna

49

Vienna Bar

North Bay

Fish Creek

Sylvan Beach

Sylvan Beach

Verona Beach State Park

Lewis Point

13

South Bay

Oneida Creek

31

13

90

INTRODUCTION

MEASURING OVER 5 miles wide and almost 21 miles long, spilling into four counties, Oneida Lake is the largest body of water nestled totally within the Empire State. Set in the heart of New York, this massive organ has been pumping life into the surrounding area since global warming melted the last ice age. From the Indians who relied on it for transportation and food and the French aristocrat who found relief from the guillotine by settling on its largest island, to the Oneida Community who found inspiration in the lake's open-ended generosity and the swarms of working men who built summer camps along its swampy banks, earning it the title of New York's blue-collar lake, this big pond has been filling humankind's emotional, spiritual, and physical appetites since the beginning of time.

It still does. Only now it's a lot easier to get to. The impenetrable wetland on its south shore the Indians called "The Great Swamp" has been all but drained, turned into turf and potato farms. Pavement runs within sight of the water on at least half the shoreline and the authorities have built fishing access sites, boat launches, fishermen-friendly canal walls and parks at all the popular bank-fishing hotspots. And although a colorful ring of cottages, year-round homes, and marinas circle most of the lake, it still boasts vast swaths of forested shoreline for anglers looking to indulge in quiet commutes with nature steeped in bird songs and the sound of crashing waves.

Averaging 22 feet deep, dropping to a maximum depth of 55 feet, this lake is shallow compared to neighboring bodies of water. But that's one of the things that make it the most productive warmwater fishery in the state. And while the cost of this fantastic fertility includes algae blooms in deep summer that streak the surface in an undulating patina for a few days, followed by the water turning chalky, the smell of decomposition wafting over its waves, the place offers a lot more good days than bad.

And savvy anglers from all over the country—and beyond—know it. They come year-round, to ice-fish for delectable panfish, walleye (called pike by old-timers, around here) and lawyers, to compete in bass tournaments ranging from local clubs to major leagues like BASS and FLW, to lower their blood pressure by casting dreams at fishy fantasies or simply to drift along and dream while watching the rod tip for communication from below.

THE WEATHER

New York's climate is temperate, averaging about 48 degrees. However, Oneida Lake marks the transition between the state's northern and southern zones, and many folks refer to its upper bank as "up north." Most winters see temperatures drop well below zero; so often, in fact, shivering locals have allegedly burned their private copies of Al Gore's "Earth in the Balance" for kindling. Syracuse averages 120 inches of snow annually, placing it high on the list of America's snowiest cities. The Tug Hill Plateau Region, stretching from the lake's north shore to about Watertown, is blessed with a meteorological phenomenon known as lake effect, in which cold winds blowing over the warmer waters of Lake Ontario generate enough snow to blanket the countryside from Central Square to the Adirondack foothills with an average of 200 inches of snow each winter.

In summer, the lake creates its own weather. A few yards from shore, July and August can be unbearably hot and humid. But on the lake, conditions are invariably pleasant.

Spring and fall are the reason many New Yorkers put up with winter and summer. Temperatures range from 55 to 65. And while many complain it is always cloudy or raining, the truth is, the sun shines about half the time.

THE WIND

Mention of Oneida Lake often brings two thoughts to mind: stringers loaded with fish, and heavy wind. This entire book is devoted to the former, so we won't go there here. But the wind deserves mention.

Stretching from east to west, Oneida Lake is subject to near-constant blows, making it moody and unpredictable, even on the sunniest days. While it primarily blows out of the northwest, the wind can come out of anywhere, turning the surface from placid and mirror-like one minute into thundering rows of foam-spitting waves the next. Indeed, the first name for the lake was Tsioqui (white water), after the words uttered by ancient Oneida braves in canoes and dugouts trying to outrace the formations of 3-foot white caps that often bore down on them, without warning, out of nowhere.

PROPER BOAT SIZE

Folks go out on this lake in everything from kayaks and canoes to bass boats and cabin cruisers. Car-toppers are generally all you need to fish close to shore near your launch site. If you plan on going a few hundred yards out, use a boat with a 15 horsepower motor, or better. This shallow lake is notorious for turning mean and dangerous without much warning. A stiff breeze can stir the surface into a heavy chop that can throw you off balance. A surprise wind, on the other hand, can send 3-foot whitecaps barreling down on you (see paragraph above), pushing you way off your intended course in the best case, swamping your boat if you're having a bad day. Be smart and play it safe; you'll fish longer.

ICE FISHING

In late autumn, wind plays a key role in setting the stage for another of the lake's claims to fame: ice fishing. Preventing the buildup at first, it actually speeds up the process as winter rolls along. Late autumn normally carries northern gales which cool the lake's surface quickly but make the water too rough for ice to catch. The wind always tires eventually though, and all it takes is one calm December night for ice to form a toehold on the bank. From then

Walking on cracked ice.

on, even the strongest blow is impotent in deterring winter's rightful claim on the water. Instead, its spray collects on the shoreline in welds of frozen foam, spreading farther out with each crashing wave. One quiet night in mid-December is all it normally takes to skim the lake's entire surface in an icy sheet, and a week of below-freezing nights later entombs the lake in safe ice for the season, often well into March.

But don't go getting all warm and fuzzy over Zephyr's role in creating ice fishing habitat. It has a nasty habit of appearing out of nowhere with enough force to blow even the most hardened ice-fishing enthusiast off the lake. Luckily, today's high-tech fabrics take much of the sting out of it, adding new meaning to the old saw: There ain't no such thing as bad weather; only bad attitude and bad clothes.

Still, even the most weather-resistant clothing and shelter won't do you any good under water. If you're new to the game, don't break trail on first ice. Instead, look for clusters of ice-fishermen and follow their path out. This way you'll know the stuff below your feet was solid enough to carry them out and keep them there, while giving you a pretty good idea of where the fish are hitting, to boot.

But if you just gotta go ice-fishing when there's no one else around, dig a practice hole near shore to make sure the ice is at least 3 inches thick. Avoid areas where there's current—around the mouths of streams, for instance. Finally, carry a couple ice picks (tie them to a string and wear it like a necklace) to help you claw your way out if you break through. The New York State Department of Environmental Conservation's website contains additional tips on ice-fishing safety.

AVOIDING THE ROCKS

Ray Margetin, owner, with wife Cookie, of Cookie's Bait and Tackle, claims "Oneida's numerous shoals make it the most dangerous lake in the state." A look under the surface of any marina would show so many dinged props, an untrained observer might argue there's a plague on them. The Oneida Lake Association publishes a map detailing all the hazards and showing their locations; available for free at area bait shops, marinas and online: www.oneida lakeassociation.org.

CATCH-AND-RELEASE

Anglers are a superstitious lot. Up until the 1960s, Oneida Lake tradition was to keep the first walleye or face being plagued by bad luck for the rest of the day. But the hippy era changed everything. Suddenly, fishing legends like

Gadabout Gaddiss and Lee Wulff began preaching limiting the kill instead of killing the limit (we're the first culture in history to embrace catch-and-release). The state contributed to the new mindset by increasing minimum sizes for walleye and reducing bag limits for popular panfish. Suddenly, even reluctant anglers found themselves having to let fish go sometimes.

Whatever your motivation, it is in the best interest of all concerned for the critter to be returned to the water unharmed. Here are some simple pointers to ensure you release a fish with a future instead of a dead fish swimming:

- Avoid going after big fish with ultralight tackle. Their long, frustrating struggle for freedom can exhaust them beyond recovery.
- Only use a net when absolutely necessary. Nets tear mouths, rip gills, break fins and teeth, scratch eyes, and remove slime, an important barrier against harmful bacteria.
- Keep the fish submerged in water, even when unhooking it.
- If you must remove a fish from the water, always wet your hands before touching it, and place it on something wet.
- If the fish is hooked deep in the tongue, guts, or gills, cut the line. Fish are bleeders and an internal wound as small as a pinhole can be fatal. By leaving the hook in place, healing will often occur around it as it rusts away. No hook is worth a life.
- Never lift a northern pike by lifting it by the eyes.
- Keep fingers out of a fish's gills.

STURGEON ALERT

The state's attempt to restore lake sturgeon into the Oswego River drainage is bearing fruit. Anglers are catching increasing numbers of 4-something-footers, particularly in the large tributaries in spring. Although its size, shark-like appearance and bony plates make it look tough, it's still a fish and shouldn't be mishandled. Females can take up to 26 years to reach reproductive age—males mature in half that time—and they only spawn about every six years. Lake sturgeon are totally protected, and it is illegal to target them or possess them. If you catch one and just gotta photograph it, take its picture while it's in the water and release it immediately.

BEST TIMES TO FISH

All fish feed most actively around dusk and dawn. Some biologists and successful anglers claim the moon influences feeding, and commercial calendars such as Rick Taylor's "Prime Times" list the best days and most productive hours. Still, some fish like catfish and walleye feed best at night; yellow perch and northern pike feed best during daylight. The rest feed whenever they feel like it.

FISH CONSUMPTION ADVISORY

While eating fish is generally considered good for you, the authorities recommend eating no more than four 8-ounce meals of fish per month from any of the state's waters. For updated information visit: www.health.ny.gov/fish.

REGULATIONS

Oneida Lake is mostly governed by the statewide fishing regulations found in the *New York Freshwater Fishing: Official Regulations Guide*, available where fishing licenses are sold and in most bait shops. The major exception to the rules is the daily limit for walleye is three east of the I-81 bridge, and in all tributaries up to the first barrier impassible by fish. The daily limit for walleye in the Oneida River is five. In addition, stretches of some tributaries are closed from March 16 through the walleye opener; check the "Special Regulations by County" section of the fishing regulations guide for details.

CAMPING

Verona Beach State Park and Oneida Shores County Park (see appendix for contact information) offer tent and RV camping from mid-May through Columbus Day. The hamlet of Sylvan Beach is surrounded by private operations. Camping is prohibited in Wildlife Management Areas, state boat launches and fishing access sites, and municipal parks.

MIRACLE OF CONSTANTIA

Up until late in the 20th century, the walleye was one of the best-kept secrets in fishing and culinary circles. Anglers knew they tasted great, but kept their mouths shut to protect their game and limit the competition. State law prohibited the sale of native stocks—still does—and Canadian sources were hard to find, so there was no incentive for professional cooks to rave about them.

The tournament angling craze that swept the country in the 1980s changed everything. *In-Fisherman*, the world's most popular angling magazine, even started a "Walleye Insider" edition, complete with recipes. Suddenly, walleye became the apple in the collective eye of fish aficionados everywhere, and now everybody wants them.

Fortunately, New York's shimmering web of lakes and streams is loaded with dynamite walleye habitat, and the state's anglers have had a love affair with the species since white men first set foot in the place. But by the end of the Civil War, the species faced hard times. Over-fishing and unbridled pollution caused fish populations to nosedive. Things got so bad, President Ulysses S. Grant formed the U.S. Fish Commission to study how to restore the nation's fisheries. The experts determined European carp, a large species with a high tolerance for pollution, offered the best return for the buck, opening the country's waters to the freshwater behemoths.

But the classy tastes of Oneida Lake's anglers couldn't be fooled. Oh sure, recent immigrants packing the nearby cities of Syracuse, Utica, and Rome back then liked the strong, fishy flavor of carp, but entrenched natives were used to the fresh, clean taste of the largest member of the perch family. Locals demanded the authorities build a hatchery to maintain healthy populations of walleye in the lake—indeed, in the state—and the first facility was built on Frederick Creek, in the hamlet of Constantia, in 1895. It proved insufficient in meeting the state's needs and a new one was constructed at the mouth of the stream, on Scriba Creek, in 1942 (even war couldn't put a dent in our love of walleye). Its first superintendent was George Frederick Scriba, whose family has had a presence in the area for over 200 years. Completely overhauled 50 years later, the Constantia hatchery is the world's finest walleye-rearing facility.

Walleye spawning in Scriba Creek.

Each April, the facility's personnel net 25,000 adults ranging from 2 to 10 pounds—a process that can take up to two weeks. Collecting 200,000,000 to 300,000,000 eggs, they add milt, stir, and place the mixture in jars. A continuous flow of water from Scriba Creek is piped in from the reservoir a few hundred yards above the hatchery to keep the spawn washed in highly oxygenated water whose temperature fluctuates naturally, facilitating egg growth while at the same time keeping the young in tune with the lake's temperature.

Most are allowed to develop into fry and are released soon after into Oneida Lake and waters throughout the state. Roughly 400,000 are raised to 50-day-old fingerlings averaging 2 inches long; and 100,000 are reared to advanced walleye fingerlings ranging from 4 to 6 inches long.

The New York State Department of Environmental Conservation launches the collection process around the first week of April. The beginning of the month is the most exciting time to visit the facility, and it's open from 8 am to 3:30 pm, seven days a week, April 1 through September 30.

But there's more.

Walleye start ascending Scriba Creek to spawn right after ice-out. Still, the vast majority doesn't start running until April. After checking out the common miracles performed at the hatchery, including the rearing tanks holding rare and unusual critters like paddlefish, sturgeon, mud puppies and round whitefish, step outside to see the natural process going on in the creek.

If walleye aren't in Frederick Creek, the little tributary that runs under the hatchery, or in the creek running alongside the building, drive or walk upstream along Hatchery Road for a couple hundred yards to its intersection with the Oswego County Recreation Trail. Head east through the field to the creek and walk quietly, stealthily upstream to the dam. If you hit it just right, you'll see the floor literally carpeted in walleye jockeying for the best spawning partners and sites. The peak run generally occurs in the second and third weeks of April. Wear polarized sunglasses to help you see through the water's glare.

Bear in mind, walleye season is closed from March 15 to the first Saturday in May, and fishing for them, even catch-and-release, is prohibited.

For more information, call the hatchery: 315-623-7311.

RETURN OF THE GIANTS

Sturgeon go back a long way in Oneida Lake. They were here way before the Indians. In fact, they swam with the dinosaurs. Up until the middle of the 19th century, the lake was so full of them, legend has it they were netted, dried and sold to the railroad for fuel. This kind of abuse, combined with habitat destruction, dams blocking migratory routes, and pollution just about wiped them out in the 20th century.

Fortunately, a few survived in the Oswego River drainage (the Oneida and Seneca Rivers merge in the hamlet of Three Rivers to form the Oswego River). By the waning years of the last century, sturgeon reports were rare but not unheard of. Larry Muroski, the colorful owner of Larry's Oswego Salmon Shop in the Port City, saw a 10-footer come to the surface (jumping out of the water to make a big splash is part of their courting ritual) when he was a boy fishing for silver bass in the Oswego River back in the 1970s. And in the bars and diners around Oneida Lake, you can still hear old-timers talking about the 4-footer caught in 1973 by a guy fishing for walleye in the channel near Dunham Island.

Still, it would have taken centuries—if ever—for the survivors to re-populate their former range in any significant way. The New York State Department of Environmental Conservation stepped in to help them out in 1993 by stocking 35 sturgeon into the Oswego River hatched from eggs taken from St. Lawrence River fish. The Oneida Lake hatchery went to work raising roughly 5,000 annually for distribution throughout the region, including Oneida Lake.

According to Carl Rathje, fish culturist at the Constantia facility, the stocking program came to a screeching halt in 2004. Viral Hemorrhagic Septicemia, the virus responsible for massive fish kills in the Great Lakes in the late 1990s and early 2000s, was discovered, and the sturgeon-rearing pro-gram was suspended to prevent infecting Oneida Lake.

Mother Nature smiled on the program, however; Oneida Lake is very sturgeon-friendly.

"They're the fastest growing lake sturgeon in the entire U.S.," claims Rathje. "This year [2012] Cornell has netted several pushing one hundred pounds. They've collected fish that had mature eggs; and they believe stur-geon are spawning in Fish Creek."

They're right. The following year, reputable sources in the Sylvan Beach area reported several sturgeon were caught in Fish Creek by walleye anglers in late May and early June; the Cornell Biological Field Station at Shackelton Point reports nabbing 18-inch fish in its research nets.

Chances of catching one serendipitously are growing greater all the time. Please remember sturgeon are listed as a threatened species in New York and must be released immediately. To ensure you inflict no further damage, the DEC advises the following:

- Avoid bringing the fish into the boat if possible.
- Use pliers to remove the hook; sturgeon are almost always hooked in the mouth.

- Always support the fish horizontally. Do not hold sturgeon in a vertical position by their head, gills or tails, even for taking pictures.
- Never touch their eyes or gills.
- Minimize their time out of the water.

For more information on this native son, check out "DEC Advises Anglers to be on the Lookout for Lake Sturgeon in the Great Lakes and Oneida Lake," www.dec.ny.gov/press/82097.html, and "Lake Sturgeon Fact Sheet:" www.dec.ny.gov/animals/26035.html.

DEFINITIONS (GLOSSARY)

BONY WATER: Shallows over rocky bottoms.

BREAKLINE OR BREAK: Transition from a shallow flat to deep water.

BUCKEYES: Emerald shiners.

CONTROLLED DRIFT: Using a motor to control a drift affected by factors like heavy winds, strong current, and high water.

CRANKING: Casting crankbaits.

CURLY-TAIL GRUB: Twister tail and jigging grub.

DARTER: A cigar-shaped floating lure used for walking-the-dog (jerked so its head swings from side to side).

DEAD DRIFT: Allowing your bait to drift naturally with the wind and current.

DIVER: Dipsy Diver, a portable trolling device attached to the line, allowing you to run a lure at greater depths than would by possible by itself, and off to port or starboard.

DROP SHOT RIG: A leaderless hook tied directly to the line, one to two feet above a sinker.

EXTREME FISHING: Fishing under unusually harsh meteorological conditions; used mostly in surf-fishing situations.

FLATLINING: Trolling a lure freely, without additional weight.

FLAT WATER: Aka smooth water and slack water; a slow spot in a fast-moving stream, usually in the middle of a pool.

HARDWARE: Local term for spoons, especially those used for ice-fishing.

HEAT: Rapids.

LEAD CORE: A line consisting of a core of lead wrapped in braid, generally used to get a lure deep while flatlining.

MINNOWBAIT: Minnow-imitating crankbait; aka stickbait.

NYSDEC OR DEC: New York State Department of Environmental Conservation.

PINCHED WORM OR MINNOW: Half a bait, usually cut by pinching.

PIKE: In the old days, walleye used to be called walleye pike, and a lot of Oneida Lake anglers still use pike when referring to them. This book honors that tradition and unless pike is preceded by northern, the word pike refers to walleye.

PROP BAIT: A long, floating lure with a propeller (generally in back) or two (one in front and one in back) so it creates commotion when retrieved.

ROPE LURE: Made from a strip of soft nylon rope exploded at the back end so it'll ensnare a fish's teeth; this lure is mostly used for catching gar.

SLOW DEATH: A hook with a kink or bend that causes the bait, usually a worm, to spin as it is pulled through the water. Normally fished with a bottom bouncer behind a 4-foot leader.

SNAP-JIGGING: Working a jig forcefully and rapidly so it jumps wildly along bottom.

SPOON-FEEDING: Casting spoons.

STICKWORM OR SOFT STICKBAIT: A fat-bodied plastic worm like a Yum Dinger, Yamamoto Senko, or Bass Pro Stik-O Worm.

SWIMBAIT: A soft plastic minnow imitation generally rigged on a jighead and swimmed or jigged.

SWIMMING: Retrieving a lure at a steady pace.

SWINGING: In fly fishing, casting a fly, usually a streamer, across the current and letting it swing back to your side of the stream.

THE WINDOW: The period running from a half hour before and after sundown that anglers consider the best time to fish for walleye in the surf.

VERTICAL FISHING: Anchoring and still-fishing a minnow on bottom, directly over the side of the boat, with a drop shot rig.

WACKY RIG: Hooking a soft stickbait or plastic worm in the middle and letting it simply flutter to bottom without any weight.

WALKER: Anglers who go out on the ice on foot instead of using an ATV or snowmobile.

WALK-THE-DOG: Twitching the rod tip while fishing a cigar-shaped, topwater lure like a Zara Spook so it walks from side to side.

WEIGHT-FORWARD SPINNER: A rig in which a metal head rides before a spinner blade followed by a hook.

YO-YO: Jigging a lure in long, yo-yo-like sweeps.

FISH SPECIES OF ONEIDA LAKE

WALLEYE (*Sander vitreum*)

GENERAL DESCRIPTION: The largest member of the perch family, it gets its name from its big opaque eyes. The walleye's back is dark gray to black and fades as it slips down the sides, which are often streaked in gold. It has two dorsal fins, the front one's last few spines have a black blotch at their base. Its teeth are pointed and can puncture but won't slice. Nocturnal critters, walleye often enter shallow areas to feed. If the moon is out, their eyes catch and hold the beams, spawning ghost stories and extraterrestrial sightings by folks who see the eerie lights moving around in the water.

ADDITIONAL INFORMATION: Walleye spawn in early spring when water temperatures range from 44 to 48 degrees Fahrenheit. The state record, caught in Mystic Lake on January 20, 2009, is 16 pounds, 9 ounces.

YELLOW PERCH
(*Perca flavescens*)

GENERAL DESCRIPTION: This popular panfish has a dark back that fades to golden yellow sides overlaid with five to eight dark vertical bands. Sometimes its lower fins are traced in bright orange.

ADDITIONAL INFORMATION: Spawns from mid-April through May when water temperatures range from 44 to 54 degrees Fahrenheit. The state record, caught in Lake Erie in April, 1982, is 3 pounds, 8 ounces.

Lorne Rudy with a yellow perch he took on a crayfish on Shackelton Shoals.

LARGEMOUTH BASS or BUCKETMOUTH
(*Micropterus salmoides*)

GENERAL DESCRIPTION: The largest of Oneida Lake's bass, this species is dark green on the back, with the color lightening as it approaches the white belly. A horizontal row of large black splotches runs along the middle of the side, from the gill plate to the base of the tail. Its trademark is its huge head and mouth. The ends of the mouth reach past the eyes.

ADDITIONAL INFORMATION: Found in all the lower 48 states and inclined to hit artificial lures of every description, the largemouth bass is one of America's favorite game fish. It'll hit just about anything that moves and is notorious for its explosive, heart-stopping strikes on surface lures. Largemouths and smallmouths are listed as black bass in the *New York Freshwater Fishing: Official Regulations Guide*. This species spawns in the spring when water temperatures range from 62 to 65 degrees Fahrenheit. The state record, caught in Buckhorn Lake on September 11, 1987, is 11 pounds, 4 ounces.

Author holding a bucketmouth he took at the mouth of Oneida Creek.

SMALLMOUTH BASS or BRONZEBACK
(*Micropterus dolomieu*)

GENERAL DESCRIPTION: Brownish in color, it is easily differentiated from the largemouth because the ends of the mouth occur below the eyes.

ADDITIONAL INFORMATION: Bronzebacks spawn in late spring and early summer when water temperatures range from 61 to 65 degrees Fahrenheit. One of America's most popular game fish, it is granted equal status with the bucketmouth in most bass tournaments. Largemouths and small-mouths are listed as black bass in the *New York Freshwater Fishing: Official Regulations Guide.* The state record, caught in Lake Erie on June 4, 1995, is 8 pounds, 4 ounces.

NORTHERN PIKE or PIKEASAURUS (*Esox lucius*)

GENERAL DESCRIPTION: This long, slender, medium-sized member of the pike family is named after a medieval spear. Its color is almost always green (some are brown), with large, oblong white spots on its sides. Its cheeks are fully scaled, but only the top half of its gill plates are. Its teeth are razor-sharp.

ADDITIONAL INFORMATION: Spawns from late March through early May in water temperatures ranging from 40 to 52 degrees Fahrenheit. The state record, caught in Great Sacandaga Lake on September 15, 1940, is 46 pounds, 2 ounces.

CAUTION: Keep your fingers out of the gill rakers; they are sharp enough to shred human flesh.

CHAIN PICKEREL (*Esox niger*)

GENERAL DESCRIPTION: The smallest member of the pike family, its body is shaped exactly like its larger cousins, but its green sides are overlaid in a yellow, chain mail-like pattern. Its teeth are razor-sharp.

ADDITIONAL INFORMATION: Spawns in early spring in water temperatures ranging from 47 to 52 degrees Fahrenheit. The state record, caught in Toronto Reservoir in 1965, is 8 pounds, 1 ounce.

CAUTION: Keep your fingers out of the gill rakers; they are sharp enough to shred human flesh.

BLACK CRAPPIE (*Pomoxis nigromaculatus*)

GENERAL DESCRIPTION: Arguably the most delicious of the state's panfish, this member of the bass family has a dark olive or black back and silver sides streaked with gold and overlaid with black spots and blotches. The front of its dorsal fin has seven or eight sharp spines followed by a soft fan.

ADDITIONAL INFORMATION: Spawns in late spring when water temperatures range from 57 to 73 degrees Fahrenheit. The state record, caught in Duck Lake on April 17, 1998, is 3 pounds, 12 ounces.

WHITE CRAPPIE (*Pomoxis annularis*)

GENERAL DESCRIPTION: This species looks pretty much the same as its black cousin, but it is generally lighter and only has six spines on its dorsal fin.

ADDITIONAL INFORMATION: Spawns late spring and early summer when water temperatures range from 57 to 73 degrees Fahrenheit. The state record, caught in Sleepy Hollow Lake, June 9, 2001, is 3 pounds, 13 ounces.

ROCK BASS (*Ambloplites rupestris*)

GENERAL DESCRIPTION: This popular member of the bass family resembles bass more closely than do pumpkinseeds and bluegills. It is dark brown to deep bronze in color, heavily spotted in black, and has big red eyes.

ADDITIONAL INFORMATION: Spawns over rocky areas in late spring and early summer. The state record, caught in the Ramapo River on May 26, 1984, is 1 pound, 15 ounces.

BLUEGILL (*Lepomis macrochirus*)

GENERAL DESCRIPTION: One of the most popular sunfishes, its color varies. It has anywhere from five to eight vertical bars running down its sides, a deep orange breast, and a dark blue, rounded gill flap.

ADDITIONAL INFORMATION: Ounce for ounce, bluegills are the sportiest fish. Fly fishing for them with wet flies and poppers is very popular. The species spawns in shallow, muddy areas near vegetation in summer. The state record, caught in Kohlbach Pond on August 3, 1992, is 2 pounds, 8 ounces.

PUMPKINSEED (*Lepomis gibbosus*)

GENERAL DESCRIPTION: This popular sunfish is the most widespread in the state. Its color ranges from bronze to dark green, and the end of its gill flap is traced in orange/red.

ADDITIONAL INFORMATION: Spawns in shallow, muddy areas near vegetation in early summer. The state record, caught in Indian Lake on July 19, 1994, is 1 pound, 9 ounces.

CHANNEL CATFISH (*Ictalurus punctatus*)

GENERAL DESCRIPTION: The state's largest catfish, it has a dark brown back, a white belly, a forked tail, and barbels around its mouth. Juveniles up to 24 inches have black spots on their sides. Spines on the dorsal and pectoral fins can inflict a nasty wound.

ADDITIONAL INFORMATION: Spawning takes place in summer when water temperatures reach between 75 to 85 degrees Fahrenheit. The state record, caught in Brant Lake on June 21, 2002, is 32 pounds, 12 ounces.

BROWN BULLHEAD (*Ameiurus nebulosus*)

GENERAL DESCRIPTION: Having a dark brown back and white belly, this small member of the catfish family can be distinguished from catfish by its square tail.

ADDITIONAL INFORMATION: The bullhead's tolerance to high temperatures and low oxygen levels allows it to live in muddy, shallow areas where other species of fish don't dare to tread. It is found in every type of habitat except extremely deep water. Spawns in muddy areas from late June through July. Both parents guard the schooling fry for the first few weeks of life. The state record, caught in Lake Mahopac on August 1, 2009, is 7 pounds, 6 ounces.

WHITE PERCH or SILVER BASS (*Morone americana*)

GENERAL DESCRIPTION: A member of the temperate bass family Percichthyidae, this species's back can range in color from olive to silvery gray. Its sides are pale olive or silver.

ADDITIONAL INFORMATION: Many locals don't differentiate between these and white bass, simply calling both silver bass. Some experts believe their numbers in Oneida Lake exceed those of yellow perch. White perch spawn from mid-May through mid-June when the water temperature reaches 52 to 59 degrees Fahrenheit. The state record, caught in Lake Oscaletta on September 21, 1991, is 3 pounds, 1 ounce.

WHITE BASS or SILVER BASS (*Morone chrysops*)

GENERAL DESCRIPTION: Same as white perch but has bold lateral stripes.

ADDITIONAL INFORMATION: Most locals don't differentiate between these and white perch, simply calling both silver bass. White bass have boom and bust cycles; one year, huge rafts can be seen feeding on the surface; the next year, they're as rare as hen's teeth. They spawn in late spring. The state record, caught in Furnace Brook on May 2, 1992, is 3 pounds, 6 ounces.

ATLANTIC SALMON or LANDLOCKED SALMON (*Salmo salar*)

GENERAL DESCRIPTION: The only salmon native to the state, Atlantic salmon generally have deep brown backs that quickly dissolve to silvery sides splattered with irregularly shaped spots, which are often crossed.

ADDITIONAL INFORMATION: At one time, Lake Ontario's landlocked Atlantic salmon spawned in Oneida Lake's tributaries. Inspecting the proposed route of the Erie Canal in 1810, Dewitt Clinton wrote of watching Indians spearing the species in Fish Creek. A combination of pollution and dam building on natal streams wiped them out. Currently the Fish

Creek Atlantic Salmon Club, a local group, is attempting to restore the species. Atlantics are the only salmon that survive the spawning ordeal. Considered the classiest salmon, catching one, especially on a fly, is many a fly-fishing purist's greatest dream. Atlantic salmon spawn in late summer and autumn. The state record, caught in Lake Ontario on April 5, 1997, is 24 pounds, 15 ounces.

LAKE STURGEON (*Acipenser fulvescens*)

GENERAL DESCRIPTION: Ranging in color from dark gray to brown, this ancient fish is long and relatively slender. Its mouth is located on the underside of its shovel-shaped snout and has barbels. It has rows of bony plates (scutes), one running the length of its back and two along each side. The largest fish swimming the fresh waters of the state, lake sturgeon generally run 3 to 5 feet long but can reach up to 9 feet and weigh over 300 pounds.

ADDITIONAL INFORMATION: Listed as threatened, the sturgeon is completely protected in New York. Attempts by the authorities to restore them to their former range are bearing fruit. Anglers are catching them with increasing frequency in late spring, especially in the Erie Canal, when they're on their way to Fish Creek to spawn.

BURBOT, LING or LAWYER (*Lota lota*)

GENERAL DESCRIPTION: Looking like a cross between a bullhead and an eel, colored yellow-brown overlaid with a dark mottled pattern, it has a single barbel on its chin and deeply embedded scales that are so tiny, they are almost invisible.

ADDITIONAL INFORMATION: Capable of living in over 700 feet of water, burbot range from 12 to 20 inches. Native to New York, they are the only freshwater fish in the state that spawns in winter. Females lay up to one million eggs at a time. The state record, caught in Black River Bay on February 14, 1991, is 16 pounds, 12 ounces. The strange appearance of this freshwater cod, coupled with its relative rarity (the only folks who catch it regularly are ice fishermen) result in its being confused with everything from snakeheads to aliens, causing this delicacy to be treated with extreme prejudice by ignorant anglers.

FRESHWATER DRUM or SHEEPSHEAD (*Aplodinotus grunniens*)

GENERAL DESCRIPTION: Overall color is silvery with a blue to olive-brown back and a white belly.

ADDITIONAL INFORMATION: Sheepshead have small round teeth for crushing shells and have a taste for snails and zebra mussels. They use muscles around their swimming bladders to produce drumming sounds. Spawning takes place from July through September. The state record, caught in Chaumont Bay on June 8, 2005, is 24 pounds, 8 ounces.

COMMON CARP (*Cyprinus carpio*)

GENERAL DESCRIPTION: A brown-colored, large-scaled fish with orange fins, it has two barbels on each side of its upper jaw. Some are leathery with no scales, or leathery and spotted with disproportionately large scales.

ADDITIONAL INFORMATION: Like many introduced species, carp suffer an image problem. Recently, however, traveling European anglers have discovered the state's tremendous carp fishery, and the species is gaining cult status. A good way to catch them is to find a spot that looks fishy and still-fish with a piece of baked potato about the size of a bouillon cube, a marble-size piece of white bread, or several kernels of canned corn. They will also hit worms. One of the most exciting ways to catch them is to sight-fish in a sluggish creek, slowly working the bait to the fish. They spawn in late spring when the water temperature reaches 62 degrees Fahrenheit. The state record, caught in Tomhannock Reservoir on May 12, 1995, is 50 pounds, 6 ounces.

BOWFIN, or DOG FISH (*Amia calva*)

GENERAL DESCRIPTION: Easily recognized by its primitive appearance, this native New Yorker has a long flat head, a large mouth full of sharp teeth, a dorsal fin running along most of its back, and a rounded tail. It is able to breathe air, using its swim bladder as a lung. Males have a large spot at the upper corner of the base of the tail. It is often confused with the snakehead, an exotic species.

ADDITIONAL INFORMATION: The sole surviving member of the Amiiformes family, a species that was around when dinosaurs roamed the countryside, bowfins spawn in the spring. The state record, caught in Lake Champlain, July 8, 2006, is 12 pounds, 4 ounces.

LONGNOSE GAR or GAR PIKE (*Lepisosteus osseus*)

GENERAL DESCRIPTION: Its long, narrow snout makes this fish easily identifiable. Spotted, brown or olive in color, it is often called gar pike because of its pike-like appearance: toothy snout (up to twice as long as its head) and short dorsal fin located far on its back, almost at the tail. Its flesh is edible but tastes too funky for most palates; its roe is toxic.

ADDITIONAL INFORMATION: Gars have been around for about a hundred million years. Like the bowfin, this living fossil's appearance hasn't changed since the days of the dinosaurs. They can tolerate waters with low oxygen levels because their swim bladder allows them to breathe air. The state record, caught in Lake Champlain, is 13 pounds, 3 ounces.

ROUND GOBY (*Neogobius melanostomus*)

GENERAL DESCRIPTION: Typically measuring fewer than 6 inches long, gray and mottled with dark spots, this slope-headed, bottom dweller has big frog-like eyes high atop its head, a large black spot at the rear of its first dorsal fin and a single, fan-shaped pelvic fin.

ADDITIONAL INFORMATION: Highly aggressive, gobies feed on just about anything they can fit in their mouths, but are especially fond of zebra mussels, worms, fish eggs, and fry. Prolific breeders, they reproduce multiple times each year, providing a constant supply of bite-sized minnows for every piscivorous species in the drink, from yellow perch and crappies to landlocked Atlantic salmon and black bass. There is no state record.

FALLFISH (*Semotilus corporalis*)

GENERAL DESCRIPTION: Fairly long, big-eyed and plated with large silvery scales, this chub typically runs 6 to 18 inches and is the largest minnow native to Eastern North America.

ADDITIONAL INFORMATION: Partial to cold, fast water, they occupy tributaries like Scriba and Fish Creeks. Although they taste terrible, fallfish are notorious for their savage strikes and spirited fight when hooked. They'll hit just about anything from worms and minnows to lures and flies. They've saved many fly-fishing trips by being the only fish to bite and the vast majority of anglers release them in appreciation. They're so feisty and aggressive, in fact, they're enjoying growing popularity among catch-and-release sport anglers and it's only a matter of time before they gain the respect they richly deserve. The state record, caught in the Susquehanna River, April 15, 2009, is 3 pounds, 9 ounces.

SPRING

1. STARTING LINE-UP: CAUGHDENOY

Fishing through the ice on Oneida Lake is about as popular as it is on open water. When March finally comes, bleeding winter out of the surrounding countryside, its torrents of snowmelt launch gung-go hardwater anglers into a frenzy trying to squeeze the last thrills out of thinning ice. Most locals, on the other hand, tire of winter by now and dream of spring. Since the lake's surface doesn't generally thaw until the middle of the month—not until early April some years—the best remedy for anglers suffering from snow blindness is the lake's outlet, the Oneida River.

Late each fall, the authorities open the floodgates at Caughdenoy to drain the lake a bit to prevent bank erosion by pack ice and to make room for spring run-off. The current generated by the river's natural flow retards ice formation, offering last minute open-water fishing through December. Still, January's big chill is hard to resist and ice usually claims most of the stream by the second week of the year, leaving only narrow strips of open water running down short stretches of the stream's center in select places like the river's source.

Fishing's easy at Caughdenoy.

At Caughdenoy, located on the Oneida River's largest oxbow, and its steepest drop, the stream never freezes. As it rounds the bend on the hamlet's east side, it starts dropping, generating rapids that the longest spells of sub-zero temperatures can't harden. During unusually cold winters, hoarfrost gains a toehold along the current's edge and reaches for the other side . . . but never makes it.

At the floodgate, the bottom levels off, slowing the current down a bit before it slides into the plunge pool beyond the foundation. River perch are drawn to the currents's edges and eddies upstream of the abutments.

Float-fish for them with buckeyes and fathead minnows in the eddies and the slack water directly below the concrete wall on the north side of the river. Tiny bucktail jigs and tubes tipped with Berkley Honey Worms or Power Wigglers are productive, too.

2. BIG BEND

Like all things, winter ages and its grip over the land weakens. The first sign of this is the February thaw. Sometimes it comes early in the month . . . sometimes late . . . sometimes not until a few hours into March. But it always comes, and when it does, it rings the season's death knell. Its run-off burrows under winter's blanket, creating gaps between earth and snow. Insulated from the last vestiges of extreme weather, warmed by earth, the snow's soft underbelly begins slowly melting, creating freshets that don't amount to much individually, but combined, pump enough water into tributaries to raise their levels, tearing apart their icy crowns, and floating them away.

Peter Scott Swamp's outlet is one of the first of the Oneida River's tributaries to shed its ice cap in this way. Perched at the tip of the river's last oxbow, this sprawling wetland collects rivulets trickling down from the surrounding hillsides, warms the run-off with its spring-fed flow, and pours the mix under the western CR 12 bridge (the swamp drains into the stream under two bridges; the eastern one has little access), about a mile east of the village of Phoenix. Cutting into the river like a warm knife through butter, its plume draws fish downstream to come and bask in its relatively comfortable temperatures.

Black crappies are the first to show. Folks from all over Onondaga and Oswego Counties line the riverbank and the short landings on the swamp side of the bridge. Most anglers try to catch crappie dinners by offering them fathead and buckeye minnows suspended just off bottom below tiny floats.

As spring stirs, it spurs other fish to come around. Anglers with a taste for red meat try for bullheads by bottom-fishing with worms, mostly on the swamp side. Sunfish claim the river's shoreline shallows and the channel running through the swamp flats, and take worms and poppers. Schools of yellow perch roam the riverside, striking worms, minnows, and small lures.

Pikeasaurus spawn in the swamp, and stick around until mid-June to fatten up on its wealth of critters; as summer heats up, they split for the river but never venture too far from the outlet. Largemouth bass thrive in the wetland, too; find its spring holes and you'll find hawgs.

Shoulder parking for about 10 cars is available on CR 12, a couple hundred feet west of the bridge.

3. MUD CREEK

Mud Creek doesn't look like much from the road. In fact, it resembles a muskrat's tail slowly snaking through a marsh; not exactly something an average angler would get excited about. But to a panfish in early spring, its slightly warmer currents feel like heaven. Feeding the Oneida River off Oak Orchard Road, a few hundred yards east of Morgan Road, its mouth draws massive quantities of panfish from ice-out through mid-April. Rob Goffredo, owner of Bartel Road Bait and Tackle in Brewerton, considers it "the best springtime panfish bite on the river."

"From mid-April through mid-May, the bluegill fishing is phenomenal," says the retailer. "A $\frac{1}{32}$ oz. Cubby Jig tipped with a spike and fished below a tiny bobber, on the marsh side of the culvert, results in the kind of action dreams are made of."

Others go to Oak Orchard for the bullheads. Massive quantities overwinter in Schroeppel Island's inside channel, and, immediately after ice-out, head for the mud flats off the mouth of the creek, where they join the massive quantities of wide-eyed bullheads that over-wintered there.

As much as he loves sunnies, Rob's bass-fishing skills have earned him notoriety among locals. "When the weather starts warming up, the weedy flat off the creek's culvert becomes a largemouth magnet," he says. "The weed lines off the shelf-drops offer dynamite top-water action with baits like Spro Frogs. Make sure to use a heavy line," advises the colorful Goffredo.

Carp action is fast and furious until the weeds choke the flat, usually in late June.

Shoulder parking is available on Oak Orchard Road. Get there from US 11 in Brewerton by heading west on Guy Young Road for about 2 miles to its end, turn left on Caughdenoy Road, travel about 1 mile, bear right on Oak Orchard Road and continue for roughly another 2 miles to the creek culvert at the entrance to the Oak Orchard Waste Water Treatment Plant, a few hundred feet before Morgan Road.

4. BREWERTON DOCK

Up until just a few years ago, public fishing access on the Oswego County side of the Oneida River in Brewerton was pretty much limited to the decaying concrete wharf stretching east from the US 11 bridge. As it got older, it began listing menacingly, and crumbling like a zombie losing rotting flesh. The authorities became alarmed, closed it off to pedestrian traffic, and built a longer dock, a floating one, anchoring it to the old wharf.

It turned out to be the best thing to happen to the local fishing scene since bucktail jigs. The south side of the dock gives anglers clear casting to the deep waters of the Oneida River (New Erie Canal), and the north side grants access to a quiet, 50-something-foot wide channel ending in the natural river bank—emergent vegetation, old wooden docks, undercut banks, and all.

Schools of crappie sweep in and out of the inside channel after ice-out. When they're not around, perch often move in. Bullheads hibernate in the slop along the riverbank, and stick around for a while after waking up to feed and get their bearings. Sunfish occupy the edges of emergent and submerged vegetation.

Author with a 15-pound sheepshead he took on a minnowbait off the Brewerton Dock.

Early on, the calicoes and perch hit ice jigs tipped with insect larvae, and fathead and buckeye minnows fished below tiny floats. Around March, the crappies' tastes change—cousin Staash claims they grow smart after getting stuck all winter long hitting mousies and minnows—and develop an appetite for small lures like plastic tubes and curly-tail grubs. The perch will hit lures, too, but never lose their love of minnows. Bullheads take worms still-fished on bottom, day time or night, from ice-out to first ice—and never seem to smarten up. The sunnies like garden worms, insect larvae, and wet flies.

As the weather warms up, just about everything in the drink visits the dock. Post-spawn Pickerel and northern pike cruise the inside channel, particularly along the bank, and eagerly devour spinnerbaits and swimbaits cast to shore and worked back to the dock. Walleye move around in the river, hitting buck-tail jigs tipped with worms and bounced on bottom by day, suspending min-nowbaits jerked or swimmed in the inside channel at night. After spawning, packs of smallmouth and largemouth bass hang out over channel drops like the one below the floating dock and hit wacky-rigged stickworms, tubes and Carolina-rigged worms.

Ray Chittenden of Liverpool with a pickerel that nailed a spinnerbait he ripped over weeds west of Frenchman Island.

By mid-May, boat traffic gets intense and most fish start leaving the dock for quieter summer range, leaving the deep water to river monsters like carp, catfish, and sheepshead. These fish grow to trophy proportions on the cornucopia riding the current coming out of the lake. Mike McGrath, of McGrath & Associates Carp Angling Services, says he's caught carp approaching the 50-pound mark, and countless catfish ranging from 6 to 12 pounds, on bait he makes from grains and syrups (see site 40 for a recipe).

"And the sheepshead," he exclaims, spreading his hands about 2.5 feet apart, "are huge! I've seen a lot of 'em taken by people targeting perch and bass with crayfish and worms. And fight . . . You wouldn't believe it!" he adds, wide-eyed.

Shoulder parking for about four cars is on East River Road, right at the dock's walkway; and additional parking for about 10 cars is across the street, next to the Waterfront Tavern's massive lot.

5. CRAPPIES IN THE TOAD

[Author's note: Different folks place Toad Harbor in different places. Some say it's the bay at the mouth of the creek draining Toad Harbor Swamp, on McCloud Road along the western edge of Charley's Boat Livery; others argue it's the hamlet at the intersection of Toad Harbor and Shaw Roads; a majority of anglers (including this author) place it at the New York State Department of Environmental Conservation's Toad Harbor Fishing Access Site, at the end of Shaw Road.]

At first sight, the title to this chapter doesn't sound very palatable. Indeed, squeamish anglers call crappie calicoe and strawberry bass to make them sound a little more appetizing. No matter how you try to sugar coat it, a crappie is still a crappie, one of the tastiest critters freshwater has to offer. And one of the best spots to get them around here is Toad Harbor.

Back in the early 19th century, when the only way to propel boats was by sail or oar, most of the shipping on Oneida Lake skirted the north shore, taking advantage of the protection its bottomland forests and high ground offered against the prevailing northwest winds. Come storm or night, ships and barges would anchor in one of the cuts at Toad Harbor, or tie-off on huge metal drums that were set into the lower cut for that purpose.

Being close to a safe harbor isn't much of a priority in an age when cell phones give you up-to-the-minute weather reports and bass boats rip across the lake at a stomach-churning 50-something miles per hour. So Toad Harbor doesn't even rank a second thought to your average boater anymore.

On the other hand, it's a popular spot with fair-weather bank anglers, one of the best remedies for cabin fever the lake has to offer. The windfalls, undercut banks, overhanging brush and trees, and the rusty hulks giving silent testimony to its nautical past draw crappies and panfish immediately after ice-out. Entering slowly at first, their migrations accelerate with rising water

Crappie caught in Toad Harbor Fishing Access Site.

temperatures, and by the time they reach a balmy 50 degrees, so many fish storm into these protective waters their activity dimples the surface.

And the anglers follow. So many, in fact, they create a colorful ring around the place. Most suspend tiny jigs tipped with small minnows (fatheads and buckeyes) or insect larvae like spikes and mousies below little bobbers. A minority does equally well—and even better as spring ages—on Beetle Spins and other small spinnerbaits, and tubes like Atomic Teasers fished plain or tipped with Berkley Honey Worms or Power Wigglers.

Some guys target mixed bags by loading a rod with a worm and fishing on bottom for bullheads, sheepshead, or whatever, and another with a worm on a bobber for sunfish.

Toad Harbor is notorious for game fish that are out of season this time of year, and you can't avoid catching them, especially if you're using minnows and lures for crappies.

The most common is the pickerel. The harbor's spawning habitat is so favorable to the species, anglers who don't understand the lake's natural order think the place is infested with them. Nothing could be further from the truth. The smallest member of the pike family, pickerel are indigenous to the lake and have been around since before the ice age. They're in Toad Harbor, in mass, for the same reason the crappie and panfish are: to spawn. Currently, their numbers are growing, filling the void created by the diminishing population of northern pike, whose numbers are falling due to habitat loss.

Pickerel are a game fish and enjoy the same closed season walleye do. If you catch one between March 15 and the first Saturday in May, it must be released without any further harm. Any other time, you can take it home (provided it's at least 15 inches long) and savor its incredibly delicate flavor.

Another species that finds "The Toad" to its liking in its off-season is the largemouth bass. From mid-May through June, schools of hawgs prowl the food-rich waters so close to the surface they can be a distraction. One angler being interviewed for this book commented: "It's hard for me to effectively fish this place while the biggest bass I've ever seen are swimming around me."

Toad Harbor is part of the Three Mile Bay/Big Bay Wildlife Management Area. The New York State Department of Environmental Conservation's fishing access site offers parking for 20 cars, a handicapped-accessible fishing platform, and thousands of yards of choice bank-fishing. Get there from Central Square (I-81 exit 32) by heading east on NY 49 for roughly 3 miles, turn right on Toad Harbor Road, continue for about 3.5 miles, bear right onto Shaw Road and travel for another 0.5 miles.

Closed for the season: Charley's Boat Livery.

6. WILDLIFE MANAGEMENT AREA BULLHEADS

One of Oneida Lake's traditional rites of spring is bullhead fishing. Up until late in the last century, their numbers were so great, you could fish for them anywhere along the lake's entire shoreline. Indeed, spring evenings, especially on weekends, would see so many folks trying to catch a batch, bonfires and Coleman Lanterns ringed the water like a band of sparkling diamonds. And though their numbers are down a bit lately, there are still enough of them around to hook the imaginations of dedicated followers who dream of the horny beasties by day and fish for them in the moonlight.

Most go up north, specifically to the shoreline shallows stretching between Big Bay and Three Mile Bay Wildlife Management Areas. Together, these public holdings cover 3,615 acres of forest and marshland, the largest un-developed area on the lake. And while the spring run-off pouring down the north shore, some of it coming from as far away as the Tug Hill Plateau, is relatively poor in nutrients, its slightly warmer temperatures wake the bull-heads from their winter slumber.

Development is prohibited on WMAs by law. Thick beach vegetation casts a steady supply of forest litter into the water, where it decomposes into a wide strip of muck. Autumn carpets the ooze in fresh leaves, creating the ideal hibernaculum. Bullheads start storming the area as soon as water tempera-tures begin dropping noticeably around mid-October. When the mercury dips to around 40 degrees, the beasts burrow tail-first into the mud, leaving only their whiskered lips protruding, and go into hibernation. Spring's warm temperatures awakens them. Filled with intense hunger, they fan out over the muck, pigging out on any worm, insect, crustacean or bite-sized winter-kill they can find.

The waters between the WMAs are extremely fisherman-friendly, too. The shoreline's combination of cattail swamps, deep forests, and high banks pro-tects the bays from the prevailing northwesterly wind, actually lifting it and tossing it out a few hundred yards into the lake, making for some pretty lei-surely inshore boat fishing.

Bank anglers have a couple hundred feet of access to prime bullhead water on the west bank of Toad Harbor Swamp's outlet (from NY 49, take Toad Harbor Road for 3 miles, turn left on McCloud Road and park on the shoulder at the culvert just before the entrance to Charley's Boat Livery). Additionally, hun-dreds of yards of relatively easy bank-fishing access are available on Johnson Bay, one of the lake's legendary bullhead hotspots, stretching from the DEC barrier on McCloud Road (closed in summer) all the way to Phillips Point.

Since the focus of WMAs is on wildlife, fishing access sites for humans aren't high on the DEC's list of priorities, causing sour grapes to gripe the authorities put animals before humans. Still, the state provides some relief for those who can't travel through wilderness, or for long distances. The DEC's Toad Harbor Fishing Access Site, located at the end of Shaw Road (off Toad Harbor Road), offers a handicapped platform, beach launching of handheld craft, and thousands of yards of bank access.

7. BULLHEADS IN THE PARK: ONEIDA SHORES

Immediately after ice-out, a lot of bait-anglers are itching to hit the open water for some serious bottom-fishing. Problem is, most panfish are still into winter fare like minnows or insect larvae, baits that are usually fished suspended below bobbers. And that doesn't cut it if you're seriously into kicking back and reading rod tips for messages from below.

Bullheads, on the other hand, are humble beasts that always look down. Indeed, while loftier panfish from the upper layers of the water column snub their noses at a juicy night crawler this time of year, a self-respecting bullhead would never pass one up. This humble nature appeals to legions of cabin-weary sports fans who find the pace of bottom-fishing for these tiny-eyed critters perfect for limbering up the old casting arm after the NCAA basketball season.

The species' appetite is legendary. Able to eat any animal—dead or alive—that fits in their mouths, the only thing known to man that is capable of killing their hunger is winter. A steady cold spell slowly shuts down their urge for food, sending them toward shore to hibernate under mud and leaves, with only their lips and whiskers poking out of the muck.

March's long, bright days raise water temperatures enough to stir them out of their slumber, and fire up their desires again. Packing a fierce hunger after their long slumber, they return to their former ways, mouths wide open. Numerous clichés have been handed down over the years to predict when their bite goes into full gear, saws like *bullheads bite best when forsythias are in bloom*, and Oswego County's greatest panfish legend Larry Muroski's *go for bullheads when the spring peepers are loud*.

"When my customers ask me where they're hitting, I usually send them to Muskrat Bay, specifically Oneida Shores County Park, one of the best bullhead spots on the lake," claims James Daher, an employee of Mickey's Live Bait & Tackle Shop, the oldest retailer of its kind in the Syracuse area. "And a lot of them come back to thank me," he adds.

But bullheads aren't Muskrat Bay's only claim to fame. The spot is notorious for attracting massive quantities of the biggest slime-loving bottom-feeders of all: carp. The window into the best fishing only stays open until around mid-June. After that, the weeds get too thick. They'll take bread balls, pieces of baked potato, and kernel corn.

The western half of Muskrat Bay is bordered by Oneida Shores County Park, which allows free bank-fishing along its entire grounds from September through the end of May. From Memorial Day through the end of August, a fee is charged to get into the main park, which offers a sandy beach, boat launch, camping, a playground, a picnic area, and more.

However, the Muskrat Bay Fishing access site on the park's eastern edge offers several hundred feet of bank access, and parking for about 15 cars, free of charge, all year long.

To get to the park from I-81, take exit 31 (Brewerton), turn east on Bartel Road and travel for about a mile. To get to the Muskrat Bay Fishing Access Site from the park's entrance, continue east on Bartel Road for about 0.6 miles to its end, turn left at the stop sign, travel about 0.6 miles and turn left into the parking lot when the road meets the lake.

8. MUSKRAT BAY BEYOND THE PARK

This bay stretches from the boat launch in Oneida Shores County Park to Fiegel Point, a distance of about 0.5 miles. Its eastern half skirts private property and there is no public access. That presents a problem if you want to surf-fish, forcing you to wade great distances from public access sites, all under the gaze of irritated waterfront owners. Its lack of public shore access is no big deal though, because the bay is best known for smallmouths, and they're usually too far out to reach by casting from the bank.

The National Oceanic and Atmospheric Administration's map of the lake shows the presence of several dumping grounds where debris dredged up during construction of the Barge Canal (New Erie Canal) was discarded. Ranging from 6 to 10 feet deep, littered with piles of gravel and rubble, the floors of these sites are irregular and bumpy, offering cover from the sun throughout the day. Crayfish thrive in the rocky litter. One of the largest dumping grounds runs right in front of Muskrat Bay.

Drifting over the spoils with minnows early in the season, and with crayfish in July and August, can result in a limit of keeper smallmouths in less than an hour. They'll also take jigheads tipped with curly-tail grubs or 3-inch plastic minnows, and Carolina-rigged 4-inch finesse worms dragged slowly on bottom. Casting swimbaits and fat-bodied plugs is productive, too.

David France, a local who has been fishing the spot for years, suggests working the natural transitions along the inside edges of the dumping grounds for mixed bags: "Generally Muskrat Bay is great in fall for bass. Largemouths stay in shallow water, in and over weeds, and smallmouths hang out along weed edges and breaks. Pickerel occupy the entire range."

They respond to wacky-rigged stickworms like YUM Dingers allowed to flutter to bottom, spinnerbaits worked along breaklines and weed edges, Flukes ripped over 2 to 4 feet of water on calm days, and buzzbaits tearing through the weed tops.

Marshall Saperstein of Fayetteville with a bronzeback that took his YUM Dinger.

Walnut Point, on the eastern end of the dumping ground, spawns rock beds that stretch out into the lake for quite a distance. Smallmouths congregate along the breaks in summer, and walleye move onto the structure during low light in spring and early autumn.

9. HARBORING PANFISH

East of Oneida Shores County Park, public access to Onondaga County's shoreline is rare. But the heavily developed area's wealth of waterfront structure draws massive schools of panfish in the spring. Although the docks and banks are private property, with access restricted to berth-holders, friends, and family, no one owns the water. If you have a boat, you can float and fish as close to shore as you like. However, you don't have the right to anchor on privately owned lake bed (marinas with man-made lagoons, for instance) or tie off to private docks.

One of the hottest springtime crappie bites on this side of the lake is Short Point Bay. Running east from the tip of Long Point (the land mass that juts about a quarter mile into the lake south of Oneida Shores) to the next point, its private docks, especially those closest to the tip of Short Point, draw strawberry bass like a magnet. In fact, Aero Marina's lagoon is a famed hot spot, but its grounds are restricted to friends, and customers who rent berths.

Equally productive are the private docks and small marinas further east. The trick is to find a seawall or natural bank dropping into a couple feet of water, and fishing the structure around it.

Buckeye and fathead minnows suspended below bobbers are always productive. In addition, small tubes like Berkley's Atomic Teasers tipped with Honey Worms and fished below tiny floats, and 2-inch Ripple Shad bounced along bottom on jigheads, or swimmed, plain and on spinner forms, produce equally well. Using a fluorocarbon leader will increase strikes dramatically.

If 15 minutes go by without a bite, move. Spring crappie are either hungry or not. So you're better off searching for actively feeding fish than trying to convince disinterested ones to bite.

10. FRANK TALK (INTERVIEW WITH TODD FRANK)

In the 12 years he competed in the professional walleye circuit, Todd Frank spent a lot of time in the top 10, and even made it to number one. He's especially good at trolling and is judged one of the best in the country by his peers. Retiring from the circuit in 2009, he joined Rassat Outdoor Group, a world leader in the outdoor industry. A U.S. Coast Guard-licensed captain, he makes extra spending money by guiding. When it comes to Oneida Lake walleye experts, they don't come more knowledgeable than Todd.

"The first thing you have to do is locate fish. My Lowrance LCX113 is so good, I can mark them while cruising at 25 miles per hour. Still, there have been times when I've spent up to an hour looking," admits Frank.

"Trolling a bottom bouncer and spinner is the most effective way to catch walleye," says Frank. "You'll catch more than you will using any other technique, but they'll generally be smaller. However, trolling crankbaits can also be extremely effective and oftentimes produces bigger fish."

"In the spring, walleyes are all shallow," claims Frank, adding "I go for them by jigging, and trolling crankbaits, especially when there's a chop. My most productive lure this time of year is a #5 or #7 Rapala Shad Rap, trolled slowly, anywhere from 0.8 to 1.6 mph. Water temperature determines speed; the colder the water, the slower the troll. Use a planer board to keep the bait out of the wake"

As the water warms, walleye head deeper. June through August, they're in the weeds, taking advantage of the minnows hiding there, the cover from the sun that the vegetation provides, and the rich oxygen supply, particularly important in late August when oxygen depletion occurs because the lake is turning over.

"I've been on lakes where the only place you could find walleyes in late summer was in the weeds. But the weeds have to be healthy. If they're brown and mossy, walleye don't like them at all," he continues.

"The only problem with weeds is you can't see the fish in there. It's all intuitive. Sometimes you'll see them at the edges," he adds.

"Good ways to get walleyes in weeds include pitching a Northland Weed Weasel tipped with a worm or leech, a worm on a short harness rigged with a ¼-ounce bullet weight, and bottom bouncing live bait on a Northland Spinner Harness. Work your offering slowly and steadily on bottom. Swimming a worm on a Rainbow harness over the tops of weeds works, too," he suggests.

"The cool thing about Oneida Lake is it's loaded with rock piles. Some are on the map, some aren't. Some are the size of a boat, some bigger than a football field. In June and July, I like rock piles in anywhere from 8 to 20 feet. Troll a worm on a harness with a bottom bouncer, slowly, 0.8 to 1.2 mph," advises Frank. "Worms on slow death hooks produce when the fish are neutral to negative, like during a cold front or something, but you have to go real slow, 0.5 mph."

Transition lines are also worth trying. Todd defines them as anywhere the bottom changes—mud to rocks, for instance, or weeds to sand.

While walleye generally respond best to relatively slow-moving offerings, there are times when a fast presentation is called for. "In August, when we get high temperatures and low oxygen levels, they go neutral or negative and don't want to do much. At that time, I'll speed troll a crankbait behind lead core between 2½ to 4 mph for reaction bites. The bait whips by them so fast they react by hitting it," he explains.

11. DRIFTING IN THE WIND

Set in a low landscape, Oneida Lake gets a lot of wind. The majority of her anglers don't mind, though, because walleye and perch bite best in a stiff breeze; and besides, it's a great source of power everyone can afford.

Drifting is the most popular way to fish. It lets you cover a lot of water, and moves you in the direction the fish are facing. And that's convenient if you're pulling worm harnesses and can adjust the weight to keep them close to bottom, and regulate your speed with wind socks or a trolling motor.

Mike Yarema, a resident of Phoenix, NY, loves to drift. But he likes to jig while he's doing it. He never casts against the wind.

"A jig's gotta free-fall to bottom," claims the owner of i 1 Baits, a company specializing in jigs, worm harnesses, bladebaits, and other tackle designed exclusively for Oneida Lake. "Always cast with the drift, let your bait hit bottom and pop it back so it hops, allowing it to hit bottom between sweeps."

He suggests using super braids like Power Pro or FireLine: "There's no stretch, so you only have to jig it about a foot; you feel the hit immediately, and the hook sets quick, too."

One of Yarema's favorite go-to spots for early season walleye is what he and his buddies call the West Bar. Located a little west of buoy 133, right in the middle of the lake, the bar gently drops from 17 to 20 feet and runs diagonally northwest. "Throw appropriately weighted jigs to get to bottom, usually ⅜ oz. or ½ oz., even bigger if the waves are really high," he advises.

This is relatively deep water, and Yarema suggests attaching a stinger to the jig, explaining "80% of our fish come on the stinger when we're fishing deep, say 20 feet or more. i 1 Baits' Tournament Series jigs come with integrated stingers."

12. DAVY'S LOCKER: SHACKELTON SHOALS'S BARS

Raised in Constantia, David France spent the best part of his youth chasing walleye and perch around the north shore. As he grew older, he broadened his horizons and took on the entire lake. Now, at 50-something, he's narrowed his scope again to a few choice spots. His favorite in early May is the southeastern corner of Shackelton Shoals.

"I usually start walleye season by jigging black and purple bucktails tipped with worm halves, or leeches on Schoolhouse Bar and Sugarloaf. I drift around the bars and jig. I start shallow and slowly work deeper until I catch fish. Then I'll stay at that depth," says the North Syracuse resident.

"A little later on, as the days grow longer and temperatures get warmer, the fish scatter and go a little deeper. I fish for them by drifting a spinner harness baited with a worm or leech right on bottom, anywhere from 12 to 20 feet deep. But you gotta have wind to do this. You can't drift without wind," he observes.

The most important factor is staying on bottom. "You gotta let out a lot of line, and attach a lot of weight so you're right on the floor. Sometimes you'll need to throw a wind sock over the side, sometimes two, to slow you down a bit," he adds.

In June, a tactic favored by lake regulars is to troll the channel between Schoolhouse Bar and Shackelton Shoal with crankbaits. Since the water is over 20 feet deep, getting down far enough can be challenging. Some do it by pulling diving lures like Shad Raps with light line, others by using floating minnowbaits weighed down with keel sinkers or snap weights. A few use lead core. Todd Frank, dean of the lake's walleye anglers, has even been known to pull crankbaits down with divers and bottom bouncers.

Still, Frank likes to remind anglers that bottom bouncing worms on harnesses is the most productive way to take walleye, and the deep waters around Shackelton Shoals are perfect for it.

Fishing for channel catfish has been growing in popularity ever since the NewYork State Department of Environmental Conservation (NYSDEC) featured rough fish on the cover of its 2011–2012 *Freshwater Fishing Guide* and exposed Oneida Lake as one of the best bets in the state to catch trophies. The deep water off the bars is one of the catfish hotspots on the lake. They'll hit cut-bait, large minnows or shrimp still-fished on bottom, or control drifted at the same speed as the current.

Gary Fischer of Central Square holds a 20-pound catfish while fishing buddy Kelsey investigates that smell.

13. MAPLE BAY

Fed by Chittenango Creek, one of the lake's most important walleye nurseries, Maple Bay sees steady streams of walleye coming and going. During exceptionally cold winters, it offers courageous (some call them foolhardy) hard-water zealots last-chance walleye up to the final minute of the season.

Post-spawn walleyes find its shallows ideal for rest and recovery after a long winter and hang around most of May to fatten up. June sees a lot of them move deeper into the lake, but some invariably hang out in the bay's massive weed bed, in 8 to 10 feet of water, until early July.

Maple Bay Bar pushes northwest directly off the creek's mouth for almost 0.5 miles. Its rock beds and weeds, especially the drop-off, hold some walleye until the end of June, and smallmouth bass all summer long. Both species come up on the shelf during low light and provide explosive action on soft plastic swimbaits and floating crankbaits retrieved steadily, and suspending crankbaits like Bass Pro XPS minnows jerked over vegetation in 4 to 10 feet of water.

Pickerel rule the weeds all summer long; indeed, many grow so huge, a lot of inexperienced anglers mistake them for northern pike. Drifting along and jerking a swimbait over the vegetation, while dragging a bucktail tipped with a pinched worm on bottom through the weeds, and drifting another rig with a whole crawler on a spinner harness above the vegetation, can result in mixed bags, and the kind of fast and furious action memories are made of.

Cousin Staash claims the bay's summer bass fishery is one of the lake's best-kept secrets. Hawg bucketmouths rule the inshore weeds and man-made structures; bronzebacks claim the rocks and weed beds in 8 to 11 feet of water. They'll take 4-inch Senkos and 3-inch plastic minnows drop-shotted in the vegetation, spinnerbaits worked over weeds and rocks, and crayfish still-fished or drifted on bottom.

James Daher, an associate of North Syracuse's Mickey's Bait and Tackle, warns anglers: "Shallow and weedy is the nature of the bottom structure at the mouth of Chittenango Creek around Hitchcock Point. Many have damaged their props trying to fish between the buoys, including me. It's best to motor out into the middle of the bay to fish. In the fall, vertical fishing for perch with buckeyes, in 8 feet of water, is dynamite," he adds.

14. OFF THE WALL: SYLVAN BEACH

Sylvan Beach has been Central New York's most famous amusement park for well over a century. Each year, however, way before your average kid even begins thinking of stuff like bumper cars and cotton candy, big, burly men are already out there, high-fiving and squealing in delight under the neon of its canal-side restaurants. The source of their amusement: walleye off the wall.

Set in a horizontal position, Oneida Lake is the state's most level pond. True to its east-west orientation, it follows the sun. Not out of its deep love of sunsets, mind you, or even because Fish Creek, the lake's largest tributary, pumps into it at this end, but because the impenetrable divide separating the Oswego and Hudson River drainages sits a few miles east.

Author hand feeding gulls at Sylvan Beach.

Still, the combined waters of Fish and Wood Creeks pouring down the Erie Canal on the south side of town probably have a little something to do with keeping the lake's flow on course. And walleye, fast-lane lovers that they are, naturally follow the current upstream to their spawning beds. And since what goes up must come down, opening day—indeed, the first few weeks—generally finds massive numbers of walleye swimming past a gauntlet of anglers, fishing rods jerking spastically in their eager little fingers, lining the walls on both sides of the canal.

Opening day is a local American tradition around Oneida Lake. Anglers start showing up after 11 pm the night before. Burley, unshaven, mainly decked out in work clothes or camo, they stand around patiently, like nightmarish Cinderellas, waiting for the clock to strike 12.

When midnight arrives, everybody starts casting. You name it, they're throwing it. Some bottomfish with worms; others drag bucktails tipped with pinched worms or minnows on the sandy floor, or swim them at varying depths; a few snap-jig sonars; several cast diving and floating crankbaits; a bunch slowly walk up and down the wall dragging plain worms or minnows on bottom; and a significant number vertically jigs Rapala Jigging Raps, tipped with minnows or fished plain, a couple inches off bottom, right against the wall.

An old rig that's still popular is a worm on a spinner harness like a Northland Rainbow Spinner, or a weight forward spinner. Retrieve it so the blades turn two to three times per second. Anything faster generally discourages hits.

At the eastern end of the south wall, between the canal wall and the NY 13 bridge, casting a chartreuse curly-tail grub a few feet into the channel and swimming it slowly up the drop-off, into the little bay, can be richly rewarding. Beyond the wall's west end, especially at the canal's mouth, guys standing up to their waist in the surf do well casting crankbaits, mostly black and silver original Rapalas, the old balsa wood ones if they have them.

On the opposite bank, the canal wall is the hot spot, too. However, its west end has an ancient break wall reaching about 1,000 yards into the drink. Anglers are blocked from all but a fraction of it by a fence, but walleye aren't. As they leave the canal, they're drawn through the spaces of the decaying structure by the warm, inshore water driven over it by the prevailing north-westerlies. Many end up heading back toward shore, hanging out for a few days in the 5- to 10-foot depths off the beach, especially in the stretch running from the lakeside corner of the jetty, north for a couple hundred yards. You can reach them by casting crankbaits, bucktails, and curly-tail grubs, from the seawall and surf.

15. FISH CREEK

The lake's largest tributary, Fish Creek is formed by the union of its east and west branches a little south of the hamlet of Blossvale. A pool-drop stream at its head, it lazily meanders for a few miles until hitting the NY 49 bridge. From there, it strikes the longest course imaginable. Twisting and turning like a sun-stroked snake, it rounds massive oxbows, splits around islands, and cuts dead-end channels. Its steep banks, vegetation-choked alleys, countless windfalls, and snags create such a bonanza of warmwater habitat that it could drive an inexperienced angler to mumble uncontrollably.

A lot of walleye go up the creek to spawn, reaching as far as the hamlet of Taberg on the east branch, and McConnellsville on the west branch. Afterward, the females storm back to the lake, but a few males always hang around, particularly in the fast water sections. In fact, the plunge pool and rapids below the dam at McConnellsville are notorious for coughing up walleye to guys casting bucktails and crankbaits in the first weeks of the season, and to flyfishers swinging streamers for brown trout.

The end of May generally finds the water above the NY 49 bridge so low and its temperatures so high, walleye move back toward the mouth, leaving the flat water to minnows ranging from monster carp and worm-robbing creek chubs to a smattering of opportunistic smallmouths and an occasional

Oxbow: Fish Creek.

pickerel. A few trout occupy the rapids, primarily in spring holes. This stretch is too treacherous for boats, but good for stalking on foot and casting crankbaits and jigs into holes and rapids.

An informal access spot is off the Meadows Road spur. Take NY 49 east out of Vienna for about 4 miles, turn north on Herder Road, then east on Oswego Road about a mile later. Continue for a mile, cross the creek and take the first right. Park at the end and follow the footpath down to the river.

Some traditional bank fishing is available downstream of NY 49. One popular informal spot is the bank running along the field paralleling NY 49 from the bridge west to Old State Route 49; the bank is about 8 feet high and steep, and the landings at the bottom have about enough room for a goat. Additional informal landings can be found at the shoulder of Old NY 49 and Vienna Road.

This middle stretch is channelized, its bottom carpeted in boulder fields, mud flats, and forest litter. While just about anything in the lake can be caught here, the most popularly targeted species are bullheads in the spring, and post-spawn walleye and smallmouths.

The lower creek stretching from the mouth upstream for a couple miles is pretty much like a canal. The water is slow and relatively deep. Marinas, backyard docks, and seawalls provide loads of fishy-looking targets to cast to. The bottom can come up without warning, so pay attention. This lower half of the creek offers decent walleye action into mid-June, as well as bass, pickerel, northerns, channel catfish, and panfish all summer long.

Fishing is prohibited on the west branch of Fish Creek downstream from the dam at McConnellsville, on the east branch downstream of the NY 69 Bridge in Taberg, and on the entire main stem when walleye season is closed.

16. MOUTH-FEEDING WALLEYE

Walleye like to spawn in fast water. Their cylindrical bodies make getting around in the bubbly water easy and a lot of them stay in streams for a little while after propagating. This preference for current makes locating them fairly easy early in the season: Find the first drop-off at the mouth of a stream and you'll find walleye.

From dusk to dawn, just about any mouth will do; from the biggest creek to the tiniest brook. Walleye aren't afraid to come close to shore after dark, when there isn't too much activity from humans or predatory waterfowl on the water. As long as there is a current stirring the drink, walleye will be drawn to its source at night.

But even the hungriest walleye isn't going to follow low current into dangerous shoreline shallows in broad daylight. A large creek, on the other hand, often has enough power to sweep weedy channels through the flats and shelves its sediments built over the ages. Walleye feel comfortable in its relatively deep inshore current, and will swim against it to pick off food riding the flow. Sometimes they're so emboldened by the safety of deep water just behind them, they'll climb the breakline and feed along the edge of the shelf.

The area around the mouth of Chittenango Creek is a popular spot in the spring. Post-spawn walleye trickle out of the stream until June. While some locals know the lake bottom well enough to drift around in the channel right at the mouth, most stay away from the treacherous weed-covered shoals and concentrate instead on the 7- to 12-foot depths out front. Casting jigs into the weeds, and jerking suspending crankbaits over their heads fill a lot of stringers.

Washed by Canaseraga Creek, the emerging weed beds in Lakeport Bay always hold post-spawn walleye. Concentrate on the 10- to 14-foot depths on the west part of the bay until early June, and the 12- to18-foot depths at the entrance to the whole bay in July and August. You'll be fishing over vegetation. Running spoons or in-line spinners so they clip the heads of the weeds produces surprising results, especially in hot weather.

Scriba Creek loads up with pike each April. Come May, post-spawn fish mill around the drop-off out front, in anywhere from 6 to 12 feet of water for the first week or so of the season. By late May they move to the deep channel separating Little and Grassy Islands from Wantry, Long, and Grass Islands (yellow perch join them). Drifting a worm on a spinner harness with one rig, and a jig tipped with a pinched worm on another while jigging a bladebait generally results in all-you-can-eat fish dinners.

The drop-off leading into the deep hole at the mouth of Oneida Creek and the Oneida Creek Bar's drop-off a little to the north give up a lot of pike to bucktail jigs bounced on bottom and to swimmed or jerked suspending crankbaits.

17. SPRING SURF-FISHING

Exhausted after their spawning ordeal (running up a skinny creek, jockeying for position, courting, and so on), walleye return to the lake with an empty feeling in their guts. The best way for them to put on some quick weight is to forage close to shore around dark.

While it's possible to fill your limit by casting minnowbaits from just about any surf around the lake this time of year, some areas attract greater numbers of walleye than others, earlier in the evening—that's especially important when the sun goes down after 8 pm. One of the best landforms to fish off of is a point.

Surfin' the mouth of the Erie Canal at Sylvan Beach.

Surf line.

In early May, the water is still fairly cold. After leaving the natal stream, walleye search for comfortable temperatures, usually finding them along the upper levels of drop-offs. They cruise the comfort zone running parallel to the breaks during day, slowly rising into food-rich shallow water as evening unfolds. Since points stick out into the lake, they generally get the first fish.

Spring Surfin'.

Osceola, NY's, Jill Jerominek, with a walleye she took on a minnowbait from the North Shore's surf.

While the shallow shelves off all the lake's points are easily accessible to boaters, only a few offer easy public access to surf anglers. They include the north shore's Phillips and Godfrey Points, the south shore's Lewis Point, and the biggest bottle neck on the Lake, the I-81bridge.

"In the interest of public safety," DEC blocks vehicular access to Phillips Point by placing a barrier across McCloud Road from the Monday before Memorial Day to the Monday after Labor Day. It's still possible to get down there, but you have to walk about a mile.

18. ONEIDA CREEK'S FALLEN BRIDGE

Back in the old days, a small bridge carried Lakeshore Road over Oneida Creek. Down for well over 50 years—(some say 100)—the place still draws a lot of traffic. Today, however, folks don't come around to cross the stream; they come to fish the deep hole the span used to cover.

After ice-out, bullheads emerge from the muddy shelves lining the creek's mouth. When the water warms up a bit, around mid-April, their numbers are swelled by lake-run bullheads looking to spawn in the upper creek and Black Creek (which feeds Oneida Creek on the northeastern side of the NY 13 Bridge). Good numbers come and go through May, all within easy reach of people bottom-fishing worms in the creek channel, on the flats straddling the ancient bridge abutment, and in the mouth of Black Creek.

Walleye spawn in the creek and trickle past the bridge on their way back to the lake all of May. Some, finding the caressing current and pickings good, forage in the stream's deep holes into July. They'll take floating crankbaits and lipless ones like Rat-L-Traps worked along the channel drops from dusk to dawn, spinner harnesses loaded with a worm and swimmed slowly throughout the water column after a rain, and a curly-tail grub or bucktail jig tipped with a clipped crawler and worked slowly on bottom any time (surprisingly, there aren't usually too many snags).

In June, lake-run sunfish swarm Black Creek, running right past the old bridge to get there. While they're available around the mouth of Oneida Creek, most storm the smaller creek, which runs through the wilds of Verona Beach State Park, offering unlimited public access.

"We'd walk along the edge and spot schools of bluegill and sunnies in the spring, and float a tube jig or a fly on a leader tipped with a trout worm; and pound them on bright, sunny days," recalls Lorne Rudy, owner of Fisher Bay Too Go, a pizza shop on NY 13. "We spent most of our time exploring the lake's countless fishing opportunities, and never had time to get into trouble."

One or two largemouth bass always hang around the old and new bridges. However, most of the creek's hawgs love the timber lining the banks. They share the habitat with a few northerns and pickerel all summer long. Savvy bass enthusiasts enter the creek silently, propelled by trolling motors, and work poppers, darters, spinnerbaits, and Texas-rigged worms and tubes in weeds, emergent vegetation, windfalls, sunken timber, and under docks.

Channel catfish ranging from 5 to 15 pounds wallow in the deep hole's soft, clean bottom; sheepshead like its steep drops. The cats prefer shrimp and cutbait, and the drum like crayfish; but they'll take all of the above . . . and worms, too.

There's parking for two cars at the barrier stopping traffic from going over the fallen bridge's deep end. Lakeshore Road South offers shoulder parking. You can get to the landing and trail at the mouth of Black Creek from the northeastern corner of NY 13.

19. TWO FACES OF CAUGHDENOY

Perched at the tip of the Oneida River's biggest oxbow, right where the river banks a hard left after slamming into a hill, the hamlet of Caughdenoy (named after the river's Caughdenia reef; "History of the Canal System of the State of New York," Volume 1, Whitford) boasts the stream's only rapids. Flood gates in the heart of town are opened each fall to draw down the lake, and dropped in late spring to allow the lake to fill back up again. When they're shut, usually in May, two distinct fisheries are spawned.

The pool above the dam becomes the best spot on the river for monster channel catfish. Nomadic by nature, inclined to hang out in current, they follow the flow all the way to the dam where they're stopped dead in their tracks. They don't mind, though, because everything else is stopped by the dam, too, and they grow fat on all the food accumulating at the gates.

Rob Goffredo is one of their greatest fans, and fishes for them to unwind after a long day at the shop. He can be found most any night from mid-May through June bottom fishing for the horny, whiskered brutes with cut bait. He's taken more 8-pounders than he can remember, and several over 15 pounds.

"Everything depends on water temperature," says Goffredo. "When I see it's 50 degrees, I'm ready to put my cat on. And if a gate's open, that's optimum, and I know I'm on the way to catfish heaven," he adds.

"I like to pack my reel with 50-pound Suffix 832 braid because it's the diameter of 12-pound, and its chartreuse color makes it easy to see. I use a 3-way swivel rig, a Mustad double-snelled hook for added strength on one eye, and a 2-ounce sinker on the other. You need a heavy weight to keep you in place. My favorite cutbait is gizzard shad I catch below the dam on a 1/64-ounce jig," he reveals.

Catfish are not all he catches. "I get a lot of huge sheepshead, some bowfin and bullhead, all on the cutbait," he adds.

Panfish are plentiful in the pool, too. "Sometimes, when I get bored waiting for a cat to bite, I'll fish worms on bottom for perch, sunfish, and rock bass," admits Goffredo.

The rapids below the dam are even more productive. On any given day, rain or shine, you'll find someone there, mostly fishing worms or crayfish on bottom for anything that bites.

Still, walleye are the preferred game down here. The gates are usually still up when the urge to spawn hits them. Walleye from all over the watershed go on the move searching for mates. They follow whatever current they can find, knowing instinctively it'll lead to shallow, rocky rapids eventually.

When gates are shut about halfway through the spawning run, fish are trapped in the upper section's rapidly rising, decelerating water. However, enough water squirts out from those loose-fitting gates to generate current and continually draw fish into the rapids, even late into May.

After spawning, many, primarily males, stick around in the plunge pool below the gates to feed on schools of gizzard shad and other bait blocked by the barrier. Anglers go for them by casting minnowbaits into the plunge pool from the bank at the foot of the gates, or by wading out into the middle of the river (when the gates are closed, you can cross the stream in hip boots) and working crankbaits down the middle of the hole. The most popular baits include Rapalas, Thundersticks and Bass Pro XPS Extreme Performance Series Minnows.

Every species of fish in the river visits the plunge pool at one time or other. Gar, for instance, invade the spot in April and May and are targeted with rope lures cast into the hydraulics created by water squirting out of the sides and bottom of the gates. Perch, sunfish, bullheads, and rock bass hang out around the shallow drop along the structure's concrete base, hitting every worm they can find. Sheepshead and channel cats mill around on the plunge pool's floor feasting on everything from crayfish and worms to dead minnows, while bronzebacks cruise the tail water, eagerly slamming inline-spinners, minnow-baits, and swimbaits like Berkley PowerBait 2-inch Ripple Shads. Even the bony water between the bridge and dam holds fish, primarily smallmouths.

An old Erie Canal era lock runs along the south shore at the southeastern corner of the Caughdenoy Road (CR33) bridge. Walleye enter the channel the first couple weeks of the season and will hit bucktail jigs. Panfish hang out in the rapids below the old gate all summer long and take worms. Pikeasaurus and bass rule the pool at the bottom of the lock and hit crankbaits and jerkbaits.

A chain link fence decked out in posted signs blocks access to the old lock—indeed, to the entire 200-something-yard stretch of state land on the south bank up to the dam. It's easily circumvented by going under the main bridge's southwestern corner. Currently, the authorities don't normally challenge anglers fishing from the bank, only those fishing from the flood gates. Still, if a state trooper orders you to move off the property, you should obey.

20. RIPPING BLADE BAITS OFF THE BEACH

Come summer, Oneida Lake's schooling walleye act a lot like our own youth: They go to the beach.

We have calendars to tell us when the beach season begins. But fish can't read (it wouldn't help if they could, I suppose, because the ink would run all over the place) and have to play it by ear. When the longest days of the year send them scurrying for relief from surging temperatures and excessive light, they head for the most plentiful shade around: deep water.

Oneida Lake's temperatures don't stratify in summer. The Erie Canal steadily pouring a river of warm water down its center sees to that. What's more, the lake grows narrower and shallower as it moves west, warming up a degree or two by the time it reaches Brewerton. And though that doesn't sound like much—bass and panfish aren't bothered by it at all, in fact—it makes a big difference to walleye and, to a lesser degree, yellow perch, spurring them to move east to get out of the heat.

Schooling fish don't think for themselves, and haven't figured out that weeds and breaklines make great cover, too. Feeling the heat as early as May, they start a slow, steady migration for the deep. By July, so many walleye jump on the bandwagon, leisure-time anglers on the Oswego County side of the pond are left with two options: settle for pickerel, bass, and panfish, or go to the beach.

Rick Miick belongs to the second group. A professional fishing guide on Lake Ontario and its tributaries, he works a lot in miserable weather. When he gets some spare time, he likes to spend it fishing on New York's smaller Lake O, especially on warm, sunny days.

"Hey man, I like to catch big walleye as much as the next guy, but I like to fish in comfort sometime, catch some rays, and get my limit, too. That's a lot easier with schoolies," he says.

One of his favorite spots is the 18- to 30- foot depths due west of Sylvan Beach.

"This is big water," says Miick. "And it doesn't have much structure. But the walleyes love it."

"Finding them in an area this large is challenging sometimes," adds Miick. "They can be anywhere, hugging the flat sandy bottom off Sylvan Beach, tucked behind the humps off South Bay [he calls it hill country], or suspended over all of the above."

Truth be told, early summer walleye are so predictable, Miick doesn't really waste much time looking for them. He simply launches at Snug Harbor, located at the southeastern corner of the Erie Canal's NY 13 bridge, and takes the waterway to the lake. Once past the red beacon at the end of the break wall, he heads northwest, into water about 35 feet deep, directly off Sylvan Beach's amusement park, and starts to drift.

The wind usually blows out of the northwest. Miick hooks a night crawler onto a spinner-rigged harness weighed down with an ounce of lead and drops it over the side to see how it's spinning. If necessary, he throws a windsock overboard to slow the boat down; sometimes it takes two.

"I never need more than two windsocks because any more than that means whitecap conditions, and I don't go out when it's that rough," he confesses with a chuckle.

When the blades are spinning to his satisfaction (three to four times per second), he casts, lets out enough line to get the bait to bottom, and puts the rod in a holder. Usually, he'll fish another rig baited with a worm on a plain harness (sometimes they want a finesse presentation), a minnow, even a crayfish (called crabs around Oneida Lake) because, he says, "I like to give 'em choices."

Next he grabs a rod loaded with a Bass Pro XPS Lazer Blade and casts with the wind.

"If you cast against the wind at these depths, you won't be able to work the lure properly; the boat moves too fast for it to hit bottom," he explains.

When the line goes limp, indicating the bait is on bottom, he snaps the rod back to jump the lure and get it vibrating, and snap-jigs it back to the boat.

This procedure is very effective for schooling walleye ranging from too small to about 18 inches. In fact, up to 25 percent of his catch is often too short to keep—but that's typical for the eastern basin.

What's more, Miick gets all kinds of hits on a good day, catching everything from sheepshead and smallmouths to carp and white perch by snap-jigging blade baits.

In fact, these lures are so productive, Miick admits: "I go to Bass Pro every spring and buy $1,000.00 worth of Lazer Blades."

Rafts of white bass, some with individuals weighing up to 2 pounds, roam this side of the lake. They seem to be more vulnerable to die-offs than other species, so their numbers are very cyclical. Some years see numerous lunkers, other years see only runts, and some years hardly any at all of any size. They usually suspend, often just below the surface, and look like walleye on the graph. They strike hard, fight pretty well, and taste almost as good—some say they taste better. They'll hit worms, minnows and anything that resembles a baitfish.

SUMMER

21. BREWERTON TERMINAL WALL

The historical record tells us that the first European to settle in Oswego County sank his roots into the Oneida River's north shore wilderness in what would become the village of Brewerton. No one remembers how he got here, but it's a pretty good bet he arrived by boat. (Why he chose the north shore is a mystery, too, considering it gets more snow than the other side.) The river has played a major role in the hamlet's economic, spiritual and recreational life ever since.

Back in 1918, when the country had more railroads and canals than paved roads, the Old Erie Canal was replaced by the larger, more modern New York State Barge Canal. Incorporating natural water routes wherever possible, including Oneida Lake and the Oneida River, its infrastructure included the Brewerton Terminal Wall, a concrete structure on the south bank stretching for several hundred yards, from the NYS Route 2 bridge (currently US 11) west to the railroad trestle. And although the waterway has lost its value as a main artery pumping commercial lifeblood into the heart of the state, you can still find everything from commercial barges and state tugboats to luxury yachts and sailboats mooring at the wall, day and night.

Indeed, the canal's economic impact on the state is still so favorable, the NYS Department of Transportation (the agency in charge of taking care of the thing), keeps the wall in tip-top shape. Only now, it isn't just maintained for watercraft. The state built a handicapped-accessible fishing access site right in the middle of the grounds, complete with a huge parking lot.

Offering level footing, skirted by a step that makes a great seat, and dropping straight into deep water, the place is just what the doctor ordered for safe and comfortable angling. Area nursing homes, facilities dealing with troubled youth, and just plain ol' folks looking to catch some fish, find the wall the perfect route to recreational satisfaction.

A relatively heavy current runs down the center of the river. It's strong enough to take a 1-ounce sinker that's been cast straight out, and carry it west so your line's at an angle when it comes to rest.

If you're itching to tangle with some of the spot's numerous bass, your best bet is to limit your casts to less than 10 feet out, and work your bait over the narrow, weed-covered shelf between the bank and channel drop. In fact, the hottest action is often right against the wall.

Productive tactics include slowly dragging scented curly-tail grubs and tubes on bottom, tight to the wall, tossing wacky-rigged stickworms on dropshot rigs into the weeds, and casting shallow-diving minnowbaits and fat-bodied crankbaits.

Gary Fischer of Central Square showing off a local pumpkinseed.

The channel is a local hotspot for monster bottom feeders. Carp will hit simple bread balls and kernel corn as readily as more complicated stuff like mashes made of grains and commercial syrups used by professional carp anglers like Mike McGrath. Catfish are partial to shrimp, cut bait and commercial baits like Berkley Catfish Bait Chunks, but will also take bread and corn set out for carp. Sheepshead and bullheads will hit worms and crayfish.

Sunfish and rock bass are plentiful in the weeds just off the wall. They're great fun to catch on poppers, wet flies and tiny jigs.

22. ABOVE THE LOCK

The 8 miles or so (as the crow flies) of Erie Canal stretching between Oneida Lake and the Oswego River is incorporated into the Oneida River. Cuts allow the waterway to bypass the stream's oxbows. The first, the Anthony Cut, is the longest and highest above sea level. It boasts the only lock on the Oneida River, about 2.5 miles downstream of Brewerton.

From the village's railroad trestle to Lock 23, public bank access to the canal is pretty much limited to the Caughdenoy Road bridge. But there's a lot of bass under these waves. Some locals even believe a new state record largemouth lives down there somewhere.

That's not as farfetched as it sounds. The canal doesn't get anywhere near the fishing pressure the lake does, and half of that goes to the old river's oxbows.

Andrew Benbenek considers this slice of the canal his home waters. Employed by Cicero's Gander Mountain since June, 2009, as an associate in the fishing department, the 23-year-old cancer survivor has been competing in Oneida Lake bass tournaments since 2001, and has weighed-in enough fish to earn the admiration of his competitors. And he's done it, in large part, with hawg bucketmouths and bronzebacks he's taken in the canal.

While other tournament anglers who fish the waterway concentrate on its obvious bass habitats, such as the swamp lining the south shore between the I-81 and US 11 bridges, the backyard docks of waterfront homes, rip-rap and canal drops, Benbenek follows his intuition to less obvious stuff.

Granted, he has some favorite sites that everyone would fish, like the railroad trestle abutments in Brewerton. He'll fish the shallow shelves around it with Senkos, and work everything from drop shot rigs baited with Jackall Crosstail Shads to jigs along its drop-offs.

When he feels he's caught everything he's going to get, he takes off for Lock 23, a monstrous steel and concrete reminder of the ugly, everyday structures that most of us go fishing to forget about.

But to Benbenek it's a work of art. "It's the single biggest fish attractor on the river. The lock's opening and closing creates a constant current that draws and holds bass," he says. "But I never go through the locks because there's always enough bass above 'em, in my favorite spot below the power lines, to keep me catchin'."

Andrew fishes the whole canal, from the rip-rap and shallow shelf to the channel's drop-off and floor.

Still, he concentrates more on the shallow water. "I look for anything that's different," he admits, "a branch touching the surface, a submerged log, an isolated clump of emergent vegetation, a waterlogged tree." The way he sees it, "If it stands out to me, it stands out to the bass."

He likes to throw Senkos. Not strictly wacky-rigged with a rubber ring, like most everybody else does, however. He'll wacky rig them sometimes, such as when he's fishing shallow, stagnant water. But since there is current above the lock, a free-falling worm sliding through it sideways doesn't look right.

"An Eco Pro Tungsten wacky weight speeds up the drop," argues Benbenek, "keeping the bait in the strike zone longer. The fish are moving and they're more likely to strike a worm dropping quickly. In addition, the worm drops straight instead of at a slant, which looks more natural and keeps it in the strike zone longer" he explains.

He also believes in offering the fish a mouthful, like a football jig with a rubber skirt. "I really get the fish's attention by adding a Power Team 3.5" Craw D'oeuvre to the rig, and working it by dragging it on bottom, shaking it every now and then to give it some action," Benbenek confesses.

The nearest free launch is the DEC's Oneida River Fishing Access Site a couple of miles downstream of the lock. It offers a double-wide paved ramp, parking for 10 rigs and 15 cars, and 200 feet of shore fishing access. To get there, head south out of the hamlet of Phoenix on CR 57 for about 2 miles to Three Rivers. Cross the bridge over the Oneida River and take an immediate left onto Maider Road. Travel 0.4 mile and turn left onto Bonstead Road. The launch is a mile away, under the double bridges. You'll have to lock through to get up to the power lines.

If you'd prefer not to lock through, launch in Oneida Shores County Park. A fee is charged when the beach is open.

23. BELOW LOCK 23

Officially titled Lock 23 State Canal Park, this is the only lock on the Oneida River portion of the New Erie Canal. Located off the beaten path, it has its own road and power plant—the turbines haven't spun since the facility went on the grid quite a few years ago. Its manicured grounds, complete with picnic tables, fire pits and restrooms right off the parking lot, make it popular with folks looking for a convenient window into the bustle of canal life against a forested background.

It's also a fish magnet, one of cousin Staash's go-to spots when he fishes the lower river for walleye during the first couple of weeks of the season. In fact, he has to motor almost three miles to get there from his favorite spot on the river, Three Rivers.

The way Staash sees it: "Walleye like a little current; if it's deep, that's even better. Water seeping through the lock, and coming out of Black Creek (it's piped under the parking lot), creates enough current to attract them. But they're stopped dead in their tracks by the gates, and always mill around for a while figuring out what to do next. The beauty of the place is that it's very narrow, averages a very fish-friendly 12 feet deep, and you can cover it with a jig in less than an hour."

"In summer, it can be dynamite, too," continues Staash. "Several small tributaries cool the water a skosh, so fish naturally stick around. It doesn't take them long to learn the lock tenders' schedule and when they open the gate soon after clocking-in around 7 am, minnows stuck inside all night swarm out, right into schools of bass and walleyes waiting with their mouths wide open."

Mike McGrath, owner of McGrath and Associates Carp Angling Services, with a huge rubbermouth he took on the Oneida River.

"Often, you'll have to cast between moving boats, but all the activity can trigger a bite. I don't know if they hit out of anger, fear or a combination of both. But it doesn't really matter, does it?" he asks.

Channel catfish also thrive in the shaded water below the lock in summer. Most are caught incidentally by family groups fishing off the wall with worms. Enough big ones are available, however, to draw trophy seekers. They target them mostly with minnows, cut bait, chicken livers and commercial baits like Berkley Catfish Bait Chunks.

If you go by boat, you can easily get on the river at the DEC Fishing Access Site on Bonstead Road, about a mile upstream of Three Rivers, and 2 miles downstream of Lock 23. It offers a hard surface ramp and parking for about 15 rigs. Get there from Phoenix by heading south on CR 57 for about 1.5 miles to Three Rivers, cross the bridge and turn east on Maider Road, travel 0.4 mile, turn left on Bonstead Road and travel for 0.6 mile.

24. EATON BAY

At a glance, Oneida Lake's northeastern quarter is pretty nondescript. Its greatest draw for both fish and man is its deep water—the deepest in the lake, in fact.

A closer look at the map, however, reveals there are some interesting shallow-water habitats in the area, too. One of the fishiest is Eaton Bay.

"The place is one large weed bed spotted with rock beds," says Pete Rich, owner of Anglers Bay, a lake-side resort offering a bait shop, snacks, and cottage and boat rentals.

"We get both largemouth and smallmouths," Rich adds. "The bucketmouths prefer the weed bed and the smallies like the drop-off and rock piles. One time my wife got a huge largemouth bass right off our dock, on a bare hook," he boasts, with a chuckle.

"Sunfish and rock bass are plentiful all summer long, and yellow perch swarm in and out," he continues.

"We also get massive schools of silver bass in the open water out front. They taste as good as yellow perch," he claims enthusiastically, adding "and the word's getting out; more and more people are going after them."

"But when you get on a school, you better anchor and stay as long as you can," he warns. A warm smile brushes his face as memories break into his thoughts: "I've had numerous customers come in to buy bait after getting wiped out, only to find the fish have moved when they returned to the spot."

25. BETWEEN A TOAD AND A MUSKRAT

Everyone's been between a rock and a hard place. Those of us who have been in love can claim we've even been between heaven and earth. And though this chapter may sound like a Mad Hatter's fantasy fishing trip to the land of creepy critters, anyone who floats over the waves on the west end of the lake regularly for fish dinners has found happiness in the waters between Toad Harbor and Muskrat Bay.

While other parts of the lake may harbor larger schools of walleye in late June, few can compare with the massive quantities of various species found in this magical piece of Oswego County's territorial waters. Huge pickerel, hawg bucketmouths, monster sunfish and rock bass all thrive in the place.

What makes it so productive is its wealth of structure and habitat. Windfalls, reeds and docks punctuate the south shore; marshes and forests, etched with creeks and springs, cling to the north side's wildlife management areas. Off to the west, I-81 provides riprap and bridge abutments; the opposite direction sprouts the lake's greatest collection of islands. Down the middle of it all, flanked by fishy drop-offs, runs the main channel's deep current.

This is Ray Chittenden's favorite spot. The Liverpool, New York resident started fishing just recently. Shortly after retiring, he went looking for something to do with his spare time. Getting wind of the hugely popular fishing seminars Mike Riordan holds at Brewerton's Calvary Baptist Church each spring, Ray attended one in March of 2011, and has been hooked ever since.

Geese on a beach.

Never one to be accused of doing anything half-heartedly, Chittenden jumped into his new passion with both feet. By the following month, he had a pontoon boat and more fishing equipment than your average angler collects in a lifetime. Renting a slip in Brewerton, he went to work honing his skills on the waters just east of I-81.

Being new to the sport, he hadn't developed any prejudices. Perch, sunfish, bass, it didn't matter. As long as the fish fought the good fight and tasted good, it was fair game. That first year, he learned quickly how to milk the spot for everything it had.

Chittenden generally starts his outings by casting Rat-L-Traps and other crankbaits into the canal at the I-81 bridge, figuring that smallmouths and walleyes always hang out along the drop-offs, pickerel can be caught moving from the flats on the lake-side of the highway to the swampy habitat on the west side, and panfish can be anywhere.

Afterwards, he heads for the massive weed beds of Muskrat Bay. "I like dragging a worm on a spinner harness over the weed tops with one rod set in a rod holder, while casting a spinnerbait," he explains. He'll spend the next hour or two drifting around, throwing the spinnerbait anywhere there's water, especially around culverts, windfalls, docks, and the bony water marked by pencil buoys.

"Don't ignore the shallow rock field behind the residential area west of Oneida Shores County Park," advises Chittenden, claiming perch, some going 8 to 10 inches, and monster rock bass converge on the area looking for crayfish in June and July. Opportunistic by nature, they eagerly hit worms, small jigs and tubes as well.

The further west you go, the narrower and shallower the lake becomes. At buoy 134, the water in the main channel is only about 15 feet deep, and it gets even shallower the closer you get to I-81. In fact, some argue one of the main reasons walleye become scarce on this end of the lake in summer is because all the boats squeezing into the Oneida River create so much noise, it drives the notoriously wake-shy beasts east.

Still, a lot of guys find them the most worthy challenge in the drink, and can't resist the temptation to try for them in the channel, especially if they're already working the weeds crowning its edges, or crossing to the other side. They all phrase their justification differently, but cousin Staash puts it in a nutshell: "Can't hurt . . . we're already here . . . got a rig set up . . . it only takes a few minutes."

Staash has been fishing for about 50 years longer than Ray Chittenden, yet his temperament is the same, he just likes to catch fish. The deep water between buoy 133 and 137 is his favorite stretch. He catches a lot of walleye by flatlining crankbaits behind lead core here in spring and fall, and a few through the ice on the drop-off northwest of Frenchman Island.

"In summer, they're tough to get," he admits, adding: "But I love this spot because the smallmouths, pickerel, panfish and sheepshead keep me hopping all day long. Hell, one time a couple years ago, I even caught a channel cat weighing about 15 pounds on a jig tipped with a worm, in broad daylight."

"But I get some big walleyes here, too" he whispers, "sometimes even in July." Looking around furtively, as if making sure no one's within earshot, he continues: "The big ones, 23 inches and up, are pretty solitary. Most of the members of their year-class have bit the jig, crankbait, or worm, and gone to a better place by the time they got to 20 [inches]. Survivors seem to like it around the source of the river, going in and out [of the stream] . . . Because they like a little current, I think."

With all his experience, Staash can easily watch two rigs dragging bait while casting another. He likes to drift one worm on a Dixie spinner and another on a slow death hook behind a bottom bouncer, parallel to the drop-offs along either side of the channel; while jigging a Bass Pro Lazer Blade, or bucktail jig tipped with a worm, with the wind.

One tip just about everyone who fishes the lake will give you is that you need wind to catch walleye—and perch, for that matter. Fortunately, it generally comes out of the northwest, so keeping in line with the drop-offs isn't that hard under normal conditions. A windsock comes in handy for slowing you down, and a trolling motor will keep you on course.

26. CORNER HAWGS

Big Bay and Three Mile Bay are the biggest dents in the north shore. Averaging around 6 feet deep, carpeted in massive weed beds, they hold the lake's greatest populations of largemouth bass. Tournament anglers know it and swarm into this corner of the lake like hornets. The bass get stuck a lot, growing into seasoned veterans by the time they reach legal age.

The larger of the two, Big Bay, reaches deep into the swamp named after it. Watered by a couple of creeks, the massive wetland feeds the bay a wide menu of critters ranging from juicy swamp insects and minnows to frogs, mice, salamanders, snakes, ducklings, baby muskrats, you name it.

Three Mile Creek drains the swamp of the same name into Three Mile Bay. Skirted largely in bottomland forest, the bay has a lot of timber sticking out of its sandy shoreline. A little further out, its floor is weedy and sprouts several humps, including a few at the entrance that stretch east, in line with Phillips Point.

Alan Handy, North Syracuse, NY, kayak fishing on Three Mile Bay.

Just about any relatively competent angler can expect to catch a couple of bucketmouths ranging from just big enough to about 14 inches by throwing the usual suspects all day long. But the big ones didn't get that way by feeding carelessly. If you want to catch a limit of monsters, you have to do something different.

For instance, rip a wacky-rigged 4-inch pink worm so fast through shoreline slop you can't tell what it is; jerk tandem Flukes over the heads of weeds; jiggle a 4-inch finesse worm on bottom, in thick weeds, on a Charley Brewer Slider Head; flip a 4-inch Texas-rigged tube into reeds and sunken timber; yo-yo a spinnerbait; bounce a darter off a log and twitch it back slowly; drag a YUM Dinger on a jighead across rock piles; snap-jig a Rat-L-Trap; swim a plastic snake over the surface along undercut banks; some guys even remove the back hook on a minnowbait, tie the line to the ring and twitch it backwards.

If all else fails, tip a bucktail with a crayfish and drag it on bottom; or a minnow and snap-jig it or yo-yo it back.

While traveling from one bay to the other, don't overlook Shaw Bay's deep flat and the humps of Ed Nick Shoal. Both spots hold post-spawn walleye and perch, and early season smallmouth. The drop-offs along the south side of the grass islands east of Wedgeworth Point hold yellow perch and walleyes in spring, and sunfish, rock bass and smallmouths all summer long. The bass, perch and pike respond to jigs and minnowbaits; the panfish like worms and small plastics like Berkley Power Teasers fished plain or tipped with one of the firm's Honey Worms. Bass, sunnies and rockies provide some explosive action to fly-fishers casting streamers, tiny poppers and wet flies in the heat of summer.

Don Sheldon, owner of Johnson Bay Marina, warns "the water between the grass islands and Wedgeworth Point is dangerously shallow and rocky. I can't count the times I'm sitting in my office and hear the crunch of prop blades hitting rocks, followed by cussing from guys trying to come in that way. Your best bet is to motor east of the islands, and come in behind them," he advises.

27. SHORT POINT BAY AND LOWER SOUTH BAY

Long Point, the most prominent land form jutting into the western half of the lake, sits low. Nonetheless, it offers a bit of relief when westerlies tear across the pond. A lot of boat anglers tuck into Short Point Bay on its south side to get out of the wind. While they're there, they can also take advantage of the best largemouth fishing on the south shore.

Plentiful shoreline structure and a massive weed bed hold hawgs like slop holds pigs. They'll hit all the usual offerings: Texas-rigged, jig-rigged and drop-shotted 4-inch worms worked gently on bottom in heavy weeds;

fat-bodied crankbaits swimmed along the edges of vegetation; suspending minnowbaits jerked over the top of the grass bed; jig-and-pigs and 4-inch tubes pitched into emergent vegetation, and flipped under docks, slop and next to waterlogged timber.

Still, the spot's relative calm makes it one of the most reliable places on the lake for throwing top-water offerings ranging from buzzbaits and Hula Poppers to Jitterbugs and darters. Fly-fishermen take a fair share of hawgs, smallies and pickerel on large deer-hair and cork-bodied bass bugs, as well as crappies, sunfish and rock bass on tiny poppers and flies.

Kyle Story with a couple of crappies he caught in Lower South Bay.

The deep weeds at the bay's entrance hold lots of above- average sized walleyes until late summer when they move into deeper water further east. While in the weeds, they'll take a bucktail jig tipped with a pinched worm and worked on bottom, or a swimbait or suspending crankbait worked over the vegetation. At night, they move in close to shore and take minnowbaits.

From Short Point to the next bump in the land, Norcross Point, sits Lower South Bay. Twice the size of its northern sister, the shelf along its bank is shallower and reaches deeper into the drink. It has more emergent vegetation— and more largemouths.

Both bays are loaded year-round with sunfish the size of a big man's hand, and pickerel as long as his arm. Crappie are plentiful around docks in the spring but are hard to find the rest of the year—some say they move out, others argue they just go deeper. Perch love the dumping ground east of Dunham Island and come around the deep water at the entrance to the bays in late summer and autumn.

The sunnies like worms, the perch and crappies take small jigs and Beetle Spins, and the pickerel hit just about anything that moves and fits in their mouths.

Loftus Shoal, about 0.25 mile due east of Long Point, is famous for small-mouths, yellow perch and walleyes. Drag bucktail jigs tipped with buckeyes, or 3-inch Berkley Power Grubs and Power Tubes on the bottom for the pike and bronzebacks; vertically fish buckeyes for the perch.

The no-name tributary just west of the entrance to Aero Marina drains a large swamp. Sunfish storm the place in the spring and strike worms or Berkley Atomic Teasers float-fished in the slow current. Largemouth bass and pickerel run the stream to and from their spawning sites in the wetland. Informal parking for two vehicles is on the shoulder at the northwestern corner of the bridge.

The biggest drawback to these bays is heavy boat traffic. You can avoid the worst of it by fishing early and late in the day.

28. BRIGGS BAY

Tucked into Shackelton Point's southeastern corner, fish find Briggs Bay irresistible. Its major features are Dutchman Island, East Isle Bar (off the island's eastern tip) and Clark Bar (south and parallel to East Isle Bar). Calved from a flat set between the island and the mainland, the bars are separated from each other and the mainland by depressions facing the open lake. Besides supporting good populations of year-round residents, the proximity of the spot's shallows to deep water draws roving schools of open-water fish to the easy pickings thriving in its edge habitats

Pat Miura discovered the bay's great fishing by accident. A professional fly-fishing guide and Spey casting instructor on the Salmon River for nine months out of the year, he hangs up his long rods in May and plays catch-and-release with bass all summer long. He's got a boat that's equipped to the hilt, but he doesn't troll, preferring the most personal form of fishing: casting. One of his favorite stages for performing his art is Oneida Lake.

Normally, launching at Oneida Shores, he heads for the bays and shoals on the northeastern corner. One time not too long ago, he changed his pattern.

Picking up a fishing buddy in Lakeport, he launched at the closer DEC South Shore fishing access site on Briggs Bay and headed for the eastern tip of Dutchman Island to get out into the lake. Seeing the crescent drop, Pat decided to try its edges. Grabbing a rod loaded with tandem Flukes rigged to swim side by side, he casts his offering onto the weeds crowning the flat and jerks it back to the boat.

Nothing.

While preparing to cast again, a fish swirls on the surface a few yards off to the side of his target, so he casts to it.

Nothing.

A couple of hitless casts later, two fish teasingly swirl on the surface a few feet in front of him. Determined to get even with them for the humiliation, Pat switches over to a suspending Smithwick Rogue. Casting out, he reels until he feels the lure hit the weed tops and starts jerking it. On the third snap, a walleye clobbers it.

The next cast hands him another.

Pat suggests his friend tie on a similar bait; but the guy hesitates.

Pat catches another; in the blink of an eye, his friend starts tying.

In the minutes it takes his buddy to change his bait, Pat lands three more walleyes. By the time his friend gets his lure out, the fish move out and his efforts lead to naught.

Averaging 19 inches, the bay's resident walleyes have outlived most of their year-class, and they didn't do it by following the crowd into the lake's open waters. Instead, they did it their way, by staying in the bay and taking advantage of its vegetation, using the weeds for cover against the sun and predators, and hunting for minnows in and around the heavy growth.

Problem is, the DEC's South Shore Fishing Access Site, complete with a hard surface, multiple-lane launch, sits on the bay. Its traffic is heavy, so you can only troll this small area during periods of low boat traffic, like during inclement weather or early, during the week. Use planer boards to keep your lures out of the motor's wake, and a planer board clip, set 20 feet ahead of your lure, as a weed stopper.

However, an old standby, a dark bucktail jig tipped with a worm, catches a lot of walleyes and smallies, too. Drag, jig or yo-yo the bait along the drops.

Pickerel and largemouth also like Briggs Bay, including the weeds inside the flat and surrounding Dutchman Island. They respond to rubber frogs, buzzbaits and Zara Spooks fished on the surface when it's calm, jerkbaits and spinnerbaits ripped under the waves on windy and overcast days, and craws or jig-rigged stickworms dragged slowly on bottom, particularly after a cold spell.

29. LONG SHORE

It's often said that Oneida Lake's largemouths act like smallmouths and vice versa. Nowhere is this more pronounced than the Long Shore.

Named for its straight bank, the Long Shore runs from Briggs Bay to Lakeport Bay. Boasting a wide flat that reaches into the lake for over 200 yards in spots, its patchwork of weed beds, rock piles and individual boulders are scattered over a wavy floor ranging from 3 to 8 feet deep. Bordered along its north edge by a weedy drop-off, and gently sloping shallows ending in backyard docks to the south, it's a 3-mile-long bass hotspot.

Smallmouths outnumber their big mouth relatives by about three to one on the shallow, bank-side of the flat. Find a bony hump and chances are there'll be a smallie or two circling it; if it's got weeds around it, there will probably be more.

The bucketmouths rule the deeper humps and the weedy drop-off.

Bear in mind bass don't really like rules and either one can hit at any place, at any time.

Since every gallon of the place is good habitat, the most efficient way to cover it is to drift along, casting anywhere there's water. Unfortunately, the fish can see you when you're over the rock fields, so you have two options: do a reconnaissance run first to get an idea where the humps and structure are located, and then sneak up on them; or simply play it by ear and make long casts to water that catches your intuition.

This is one of Wes Coy's favorite spots. A bass tournament angler who describes himself as a "Jerk on one end of the line waiting for a jerk on the other," he often determines strategy for the day's competition by motoring out about 100 yards or so off the Long Shore, catching the wind, and drifting along, casting attractor baits to see what the fish are into that day.

One of his most productive techniques is drop-shotting a 3-inch Senko, in

Wes Coy thanking a bronzeback.

shallow water, no less. He does it by casting great distances. The guy's got the eye of a Marine Corp sniper, able to hit a dock's upright with a sinker from 50 feet away.

He also likes to keep a wacky-rigged Bass Bone handy. It's one of his go-to lures when his imagination nags at him that there's still a bass in a spot that he's covered with the drop shot.

Spinnerbaits are extremely effective in the shallows, too, taking a big bite out of the Long Shore's bass community during tournaments. Bass are conservative pillars of the aquatic community. Seeing one of the flashy contraptions noisily ripping through the neighborhood is enough to make a self-respecting hawg see red and strike at its tormentor. Monster rock bass and sunfish love the Long Shore, too. The rockies can't resist a wacky-rigged YUM Dinger fluttering to bottom, and the sunnies like worms. Unfortunately, round gobies have colonized the lake and you'll get five for every pumpkinseed. You can avoid much of the aggravation by targeting the panfish with tiny marabou jigs, tubes and 1-inch curly-tail grubs.

30. LAKEPORT BAY

Lakeport Bay is the fishy equivalent of a mountain resort. Fed by Canaseraga Creek, its cool waters offer comfort when the rest of the lake is sweating under sweltering temperatures. So, about the only way a fish ever leaves the place is at the end of a stringer.

That happens quite a bit. As anyone who likes a fish sandwich can tell you, a cool fish is a tasty fish. The lake's savviest subsistence anglers know it, hit the spot regularly, and protect its privacy like members of a secret society.

With everything the bay's got going for it, you wouldn't think they'd be worried about their favorite spot getting fished out. And they're not. What they're trying to avoid is crowds. As Cousin Staash likes to say: "Lakeport Bay gets awfully small when you have two or three boats on it."

The second thing that attracts and holds fish is a massive weed bed. Walleye and perch find cover from the bright sun in the shadows along the edges. The pike strike bucktail jigs tipped with worms and bounced gently along the floor; floating jigheads on three-way swivel rigs drifted with the wind, and worms on harnesses, spinner-rigged and plain, dragged slowly on bottom. Perch will hit the same stuff, but are especially fond of small minnows fished on bottom off drop-shot rigs.

Fishing in the grass is challenging but also productive. Texas-rigged worms dropped into weed openings, edges, even into the thick of things, and jiggled teasingly on bottom; 4-inch finesse worms rigged on Charlie Brewer Slider Heads and gently jigged in the weeds; and drop-shotted 3-inch worms shaken along weed edges can result in so many smallies, you won't be able to wipe the smile off your face until morning.

Surface baits are effective on calm days. Buzzbaits ripped over weeds, walking-the-dog with darters around structure and windfalls, and running spoons so they wobble just below the surface, can trigger such explosive action from bass, northern pike, pickerel and an occasional walleye, you'll think you strayed into a mine field.

Sunnies reach memorable proportions in this fish-friendly habitat, and strike every night crawler they can find.

Still, the most exciting top-water lures to use are bass bugs. In fact, this spot is perfect for learning how to fly-fish with poppers and hair bugs.

"Hawg bass are the most conservative fish in the drink," says Cousin Staash. "The racket of a big bug chugging and spitting on the surface is enough to cause 'em to see red. But when the bug stops and rests motionless for a few seconds, then starts making noise again, it'll charge the lure to kill it. The strike is so violent it'll straighten out both your arms."

"Even more exciting," Staash adds "is taking one out of lily pads. I like to cast my popper onto the third or fourth pad in, let it sit for a moment, and then skip it to the pad in front of it. If there's a bass under there, he'll generally come out to the edge of the plants to investigate what's jumping on his roof. When you twitch the rod tip again to send the lure into the water, the bass'll hit it so violently, its spray will get you all wet."

The strikes Staash describes above are from smallmouths. Largemouths are usually bigger, and make a greater splash. While the bay boasts a small population, their numbers should increase in the future.

Frank Flack, fisheries biologist with NYSDEC Region 6, explains: "Since the appearance of zebra mussels in the early nineties, weed growth is spreading deeper and deeper into the lake, favoring the spread of largemouth bass."

Considering the west end of the lake already boasts about the best trophy bucketmouth fishing you can expect in a lake that freezes-over three months out of the year, this development promises to make Oneida Lake one of the best bass spots on the planet.

31. BOTTOM FEEDING AT CLEVELAND DOCK

Barely larger than a brook, Black Creek packs an awfully powerful punch for a stream its size. Over the millennium, it's patiently dug a deep channel at its mouth. Gouging out the rocks and sand in its way with forest debris carried off the Tug Hill Plateau, it piled the stuff into a point reaching out of its west bank. Early in the 19th century, an economic boom swept over the north shore, giving birth to the hamlet of Cleveland. Village fathers took advantage of the point's natural harbor by building a wharf along its east side to facilitate shipment of local products ranging from lumber to glass.

Having seen its share of good times and bad, the grounds of the modest port are currently enjoying a renaissance. Only today, instead of fueling the industrial revolution, Cleveland Dock is a NYSDEC-run public fishing access site, complete with a bait shop and parking for about 15 cars, on the north shore's most productive bank-fishing hotspot for summer bottom feeders.

Sitting on the widest part of the lake, roughly a mile north of its deepest spot, Cleveland Dock is blessed with two fish magnets: Black Creek and deep water right at the wall. While more popular areas like Sylvan Beach and Brewerton boast greater current and more bank-fishing access, the quality of their fishing experience doesn't come close to that at the dock. You see, the Erie Canal runs through both, carrying partyers, mechanical noises and the smell of fuel by day; and dueling boat lights at night. Not that that's a bad thing—after all, some anglers enjoy fishing in a resort atmosphere. But if you're looking for a quality bank-fishing trip steeped in the natural sights and sounds of Oneida Lake, set in a colorful tapestry of quaint waterfront structures, Cleveland Dock is the place to go.

Perched on top of the old concrete wharf, this site is about as tranquil and scenic as they come. Breakwaters on the east and west approaches discourage recreational boat traffic from running too close to shore. To the north, an ancient light, built of sheet metal painted barn-red, sits in the corner of a private marina ringed in leaning docks with warped decking. And although NY 49 runs within casting distance of the water, and Apps Landing rents slips, so boats come and go throughout the day, neither generates enough traffic to foul the air, let alone disturb the peace and quiet of the place.

The fishing is laid back, too. For the most part, the daytime bite isn't extraordinary. And the regulars don't seem to mind.

The most popular bait is a worm fished on bottom. On a warm summer day, the luckiest anglers catch enough sheepshead, yellow perch and rock bass to feed a family of four. Occasionally, especially at dusk, dawn and on cloudy days, bullheads and channel catfish bite-up a storm. Schools of cookie-cutter smallies ranging from too small to just big enough invade the place regularly.

But there's a lot of big fish, too, like trophy channel catfish and sheepshead the size of trash can lids. Monster carp up to 50 pounds cruise the north shore shallows and find the dock's deep water comforting on beautiful days when the open lake is swamped in peak boat traffic.

Serious trophy seekers consider the dock a must-stop. Weeds at the western entrance and along the north shore are home to pickerel and panfish. Rock fields, especially the ones clinging to the sides of the breakwaters, support

Mark Davis, Westmoreland, NY, holding a 13-pound Oneida Lake Kitty.

monster resident bronzebacks. Non-schooling walleye—the 21- to 25-inch survivors of year classes that have been whittled down over the years by fishing pressure—stalk prey in the dark depths. And hawg bucketmouth always prowl the harbor's structures. In fact, each year spawns numerous stories among the bank-fishing crowd of "the hawg bass taken by some guy throwing lures along the wall."

Summer's best fishing occurs after a thunderstorm swells Black Creek to twice its normal size, or better. Its murky plume, driven by run-off and loaded with worms and insects swept off the land, slices deep into the lake, drawing open-water catfish, yellow perch and walleye to the cornucopia pouring out of its mouth.

32. BUOY BOUNCING

Cousin Staash, a guy whose wife describes him as "a lazy do-nuthin' who fishes too much," likes to "buoy bounce": break the day into three or four two-hour segments, each devoted to fishing around a specific buoy.

Buoy bouncing is especially popular with guys who fish the old way, without electronics. While triangulation can help locate open water structure, it's an iffy process often requiring several passes over an area to locate the desired spot. Buoys, on the other hand, are easy to find and often mark the spot.

For instance, buoy 133 sits on the drop-off that runs along the north side of Frenchman and Dunham Islands. Buoy 130, about 0.5 mile due south of Long Island, sits in the middle of the north edge of a canal-cut between two bars, a late summer hot spot for yellow perch. Buoy 125 sits on the northern drop-off on Shackelton Shoal's west side; Buoy 123 is centered on the shoal's north edge—on a bar rising from the drop-off; and Buoy 121 marks the eastern end of the shoal—Big Isle, Sugar Loaf and Newfoundout

Capt. Rick Miick buoy bouncing.

on High Bar, respectively, are south of it. Buoy 113, marks Messenger Shoal, the only meaningful off-shore structure on the east end of the lake, and a year-round hot-spot for walleye, yellow perch, smallmouths and silver bass.

33. PANCAKES FOR BREAKFAST . . . OR ANY OTHER TIME

Oneida Lake looks like a fallen bottle. Its west side is narrow, shallow, and boasts most of the weed beds. The east side is wide, soft-bottomed and has all the deep spots. What the east side lacks in vegetative cover, it more than makes up for in Oneida Lake pancakes; source of some of the lake's greatest food sources.

About the size and shape of hot cakes, these nodules of iron and manganese carpet vast stretches of bottom, in 25 to 35 feet of water, mostly on the gentle drop-offs around mid-lake shoals. The slopes around Dakin and Shackelton Shoals are known for the things. In fact, current fishing maps show a Pancake Shoal west of Dakin, and older maps also name the bar two miles north of Lakeport Bay as Pancake Shoal. While place names can come and go, one Oneida Lake saying is here to stay: Find pancakes and you'll find game fish.

Although they're named after one of America's favorite breakfast foods, flavor has nothing to do with their popularity among the lake's game fish. What draws them to the pancakes are schools of white and yellow perch minnows that feed on scuds, freshwater shrimp that thrive around these formations.

"I believe the whole end of Shackelton Point is pancakes," says Lorne Rudy, "and schools of walleye are always hanging around. The trick to fishing pancakes is moving . . . drifting or trolling to stay on top of the fish," he adds.

From May through July, most anglers drift and jig bucktails tipped with worms, Jigging Raps fished plain or tipped with minnows or XPS Lazer Blades on one side of the boat, and run worms on bottom, off harnesses or spinner-rigs, on the other side. Equally productive is trolling minnow-baits like Smithwick Rogues, XPS Extreme Minnows or Jr. Thundersticks off divers, a foot or two off bottom.

34. BLADE RUNNING ON SHACKELTON SHOALS

Shackelton is the most famous shoal on the lake—mostly because it's the biggest. Stretching for roughly 2.5 miles from east to west, and 0.75 mile from north to south, it's sunk almost smack in the middle of the lake. Rising from depths averaging 37 feet, it can come to less than a foot below the surface (depending on how high the lake is) on its east end, close enough to to kiss the bottom of your boat.

Seasoned salts like Capt. Rick Miick place the shoals in their favorites column "because there's always walleye around." The colorful New Jersey expatriate came up to the Salmon River some 20 years ago, fell in love with Central New York's woods and waters—and his wife-to-be—and settled in. In about the time it takes a coho to mature, he started Dream Catcher Charters and Guide Service, and has been making a living on the world famous eastern corner of the tiniest Great Lake ever since. When he's looking for a break from the "same-o, same-o" of guiding on the big pond and its tributaries, or starring in fishing programs like "The Run," "Reel Monster TV" and "Team E Outdoors," he heads south to Oneida Lake and aims his bow for Shackelton Shoals.

Early in the season, walleye are on the shoals looking for warm temperatures and can be taken on jigs tipped with worms and crankbaits like XPS Extreme Minnows worked in less than five feet of water, even on sunny days.

But as the days get longer and brighter, you have to go deeper. By late July, Miick can find himself working bottom in water over 30 feet deep. His favorite spot at this time is between Buoy 121 and 123. Walleye can invade the 10- to 30-foot depths in such numbers, on the monitor they look like a carpet below arched chandeliers suspended from an invisible ceiling.

"From opening day through the middle of July, I like to jig ⅝ oz. Bass Pro's Lazer Blades in perch," says Miick. "I prevent the hooks from tangling during the cast by stopping at the end of the back-swing, and resuming the cast very forcefully when they stop swinging. Jig the bladebait slowly, allowing it to drop to bottom after every jerk. Work it all the way to the boat—you wouldn't believe how many times they hit right at the side," he advises.

"The most important thing is to cast with the wind," claims Miick. "This way you can make sure the bait hits bottom and you can control its speed."

"I increase my chances of scoring by always fishing a worm on a slowdeath hook, and another on a spinner-harness on the other side of the boat," he adds. "You have to move your head a lot to keep up with things but it's worth it."

One of the shoal's features that Miick likes to fish is what he calls "the rolling hills," humps on the south side, between the buoys.

Miick says the pickings are best until the end of June, and again from late September into November. Mid- to late summer is good, too, but the bite begins slowing down tremendously in August when the year's newly hatched gizzard shad reach 1- to 2-inches long, giving the pike more food than they know what to do with. The bait is so abundant by the end of the month, and the walleye so full, that some of the lake's most famous anglers won't go out between the second week of August and the first week of September for fear of getting skunked.

35. JIGGIN' SHACKELTON SHOALS

When the bite gets tough, the tough get creative. Lorne Rudy claims: "I learned a long time ago that from late August into September, in the dog days of summer, when the lake is turning over and everything in the place has lock jaw, walleye will sometimes hit one of the perch's favorite dishes, crayfish."

It's hard to argue with him because he has some impressive credentials. Raised on Billington Bay, on the west side of Shackelton Point, the colorful pizza chef has been fishing the area for over 30 years. His grandfather, George Rudy, used to take him to his favorite bass spot, Eel Isle, and taught him how to back-hook a crayfish on a jighead and work the car-size boulders on the bony hump 0.5 mile due north of Hitchcock Point.

Now, Loren likes to catch bass as much as the next guy, but he loves to eat walleye and perch. As he—and gramps—got older, the youngster had to find new fishing buddies, and began exploring the lake's possibilities with kids his age. Curious and eager to experiment, they learned how to find early-season walleye between the mainland and the shoal by running at right angles to shore. "When we found the line of pike, we'd troll through them from east to west; flatlining Thundersticks and Rapalas if they were shallow, off divers when they were deep," says Rudy.

As the season heated up into the dog days of summer, Lorne often found himself fishless, desperate. So he tried grandpa's jig-and-crayfish combo on his favorite spot: the Shackelton Cuts, the relatively steep drop caused by the lake's contour lines tightening about 0.25 mile north of Shackelton Point. And it worked; not only on the smallies, but also the perch and, more importantly, walleye.

Seeing how well walleye responded to crayfish, Lorne experimented. Before long, he claims he was catching summer walleye by working a jig-rigged crayfish with the wind on one side of the boat, and drifting a back-hooked crayfish on a spinner harness, behind enough weight to get it to bottom, on the other side.

"Windy days are best, especially if it's blowing out of the north or west," he advises, reasoning: "the fish are normally scattered, so you have to drift over a lot of water to find them, and it stirs things up, blowing food toward the south shore. In fact, the only times I'm reluctant to go out is when there's no wind or when there's too much. Use a wind sock to slow you down."

36. JOE'S PLACE

The gently sloping bottom off Larkin and Bushnell Points sprouts a small shoal about half way between them. Located about 100 yards out, off the Lake Oneida Beach Association's Syracuse Herald Ave, it's right in front of Joe Lampreda's camp. Joe's grandfather got the property in the early part of the last century when the Syracuse Herald newspaper tried increasing its circulation by offering small lots on installment to subscribers.

He's been fishing the place ever since he can remember, and fondly reminisces how he, his dad and granddad flatlined Rapalas in May and June, and in autumn, along the outside drop for walleye. "We used to get some pretty big ones, too," he adds, "23-inchers, even better."

Nowadays, Joe continues the family tradition with his daughter, Lindsay.

In summer, the spot is crowned in a dynamite weed bed, becoming the haunt for smallies, pickerel and panfish. The game fish respond to surface plugs like poppers and buzzbaits cast over the vegetation on calm days, and to Texas-rigged worms and finesse worms on Charley Brewer's Slider Heads worked on bottom in the weeds. Drag a worm on a jighead or spinner harness for the panfish.

37. FISHIN' DOGS: GARY AND KELSEY

Central Square's Gary Fischer never goes fishing without Kelsey, his golden retriever. She's his second most important duck hunting accessory—after his gun. She can sit at the bottom of the boat silently, motionless, for hours and Gary likes to think he trained her to do that. But when you watch her closely, and see how she sways with the waves without falling asleep, keeping her eyes peeled on everything that comes into view, it's obvious she's bird watching, not just there for the ride.

Gary likes to troll. In July and August, he does pretty good fishing the short bar about 0.25 mile south the New York State Department of Environmental Conservation's Godfrey Point fishing access site (1.5 miles east of the hamlet of Cleveland on NY 49). Submerged under 12 feet of water, rising out of 17 feet of water to the north and 40 feet to the south, the structure is favored by schooling walleye and perch.

He likes to get there early in the morning but says dusk is a good time, too. His most productive technique is using a three-way swivel rig to troll a floating jighead tipped with a night crawler along the outside drop-off, in anywhere from 20 to 30 feet of water; concentrating on the deep end during daylight, and climbing higher in fading light.

Kelsey's first algae bloom.

38. MUD LINES

Oneida's temperature doesn't stratify in summer; heavy winds, tributaries and the New Erie Canal continuously stir it up, preventing a thermocline from forming. With temperatures pretty much the same throughout the lake, fish are mostly drawn to deep water in search of security, relief from the scorching sun, and the food-rich pancakes carpeting the floor.

However, a variety of factors can send them back into shallower water in deep summer. Oxygen depletion caused by spells of hot, dry and calm weather, for instance, and mud lines created by storm run-off.

Heavy rains swell tributaries with muddy water, sending their colored plumes deep into the lake. Carrying terrestrial goodies like insects and worms, providing ideal cover for minnows, the soiled water is a veritable cornucopia, hooking the appetites of predators, leading them to its source.

Wind pushes the streams' currents against the shore; a north blow wraps the south shore near creek mouths in ribbons of turbidity, while a south blow sends streaks of murky currents running parallel to the north shore. Emboldened by the sense of security that low visibility provides, walleye dart in and out, picking off food (lateral lines allow pike to feel vibrations caused by the movement of minnows and other life forms, so they don't need to see their prey).

Canaseraga Creek creates one of the most consistently prominent mud lines. North and west winds push it against the south shore from its mouth in the heart of Lakeport all the way to Bushnell Point, a distance of over a mile. Drift along the color line with worm harnesses, while casting a bucktail jig or rattling minnowbait tight to the murky edge, as well as into the stained flow.

Fishing a mud line.

Another great spot is Black Creek at Cleveland Dock. The deep shelf due south of the terminal wall holds walleye and bass year-round. When the stream runs high and stained with run-off, it lures predators tight to the dock. Jigging a bucktail tipped with a clipped worm, a Berkley Power Wiggler or Honey Worm (for flavor, you see), through the soiled plume, can result in a walleye or two stretching the tape at over 20 inches. The bronzebacks will hit the jig, too, but seem to prefer tubes and Carolina-rigged plastic worms.

During a west wind, Oneida Creek's plume is pushed along the east shore, over Oneida Creek Bar and the relatively steep, inshore drop-off stretching north past Verona Beach State Park. This corner of the lake is relatively featureless and the stained water draws walleye wandering over the sandy floor up to the shallow shelf skirting the shoreline. Run minnowbaits and swimbaits along the edge of the drop-off.

39. SMALLIES IN THE HEAT

Professional bass angler Wes Coy (no relation to Wiscoy Creek near Rochester) loves Oneida Lake's smallmouths. He knows the largemouths grow bigger but he feels smallies are scrappier and a lot more fun to catch. He's hugely successful, catching his limit of chunky bronzebacks virtually every time out and consistently scoring high at weigh-ins during local bass tournaments.

And he does it when he wants to, even in August, when most guys hang up their fishing tackle until the weather cools down in mid-September. While others are staying home, reasoning everything is blooming and there's too much food around for the fish to cooperate, Wes is out catching his limits of some of the fattest bass of the year.

Asked how he does it, he replies quickly, "I milk run. Most of the rest of the year I'll work a spot for all its worth," he explains. "But in deep summer, you have to be flexible. If they're not hitting in an area, don't keep pounding it stubbornly like you think you're going to force a bite. Instead, do like a milk delivery guy in the old days: travel around, stopping for a few casts in every likely spot until you find a school of cooperative bass. Sometimes I have to run for 10 miles before scoring."

Normally, deep summer finds him launching at the New York State Department of Environmental Conservation's South Shore Fishing Access Site (2 miles east of Bridgeport on NY 31). Wes begins by working what he calls the Long Shore, the flat between the boat launch and Lakeport Bay. He stays close to shore, drop shotting a three-inch Senko in the weeds, under docks, alongside boulders and over rock fields. He doesn't drop shot conventionally by pitching close to the boat. Instead, he casts long distances into three to five feet of water.

"I like to use a three-inch Senko on my drop shot rig because it's different. Smallies react better to strange baits when there's a lot of food around."

If he comes up blank, he shifts to deeper water, primarily the outer edges of weed beds around humps and shoals, anywhere he finds extreme changes in bottom. He'll head for Dunham Island and work the edges of the weed beds, the channel's drop-offs, even the "sunken Newspaper Barge" by drifting and casting the same drop- shot rig anywhere from the treacherous shallows below the pencil buoys to the 18-foot depths 150 yards further north.

On days when the fish still aren't hitting, he takes drastic measures and runs across the lake, a distance of five miles, to Eaton Shoals on the east side of Cleveland, and works his drop-shot magic in weeds and along breaks.

If that doesn't work, he'll try Vienna Bar, Messenger Shoal, maybe even the canal at Sylvan Beach, going wherever he has to catch a fish.

40. END CAST AT THE RIVERHEAD

While there's no shortage of reasons to criticize government, sometimes you have to give it a little credit, too. And that's easy when it comes to all the wonderful fishing access sites the NYSDEC maintains around the lake. Two that get more than their fair share of summer use sit at the source of the Oneida River, right below I-81.

The easiest one to get to, and fish from, is on the north side of the bridge, off CR 37 (from I-81 exit 31, Brewerton, head west on Bartel Road for about 0.5 mile, turn right at the light onto US 11, cross the bridge, turn right at the next light, and continue for about 0.5 mile to the FAS parking lot on the east side of the interstate's overpass). The site has room for about 25 cars, and offers a level, roughly 100-yard-long, paved path to the water. A handicapped- accessible fishing platform reaches out of the bridge abutment like a wrap-around porch.

At its west bank, the lake is funneled into the Oneida River. Averaging 14 feet deep, swept by a strong current, the bottleneck draws fish from all over this half of the lake. Panfish worth writing home about, monster channel cats and carp, sheepshead broader than garbage can lids, hawg bucketmouths and smallies, all come around at one time or another, with many hanging out year-round.

Walleye move in and out of the river from opening day through early July. A surprising number are caught in the deep channel right off the fishing platform, in broad daylight, on bucktail jigs tipped with pieces of worm, and on night crawlers on spinner harnesses, dragged slowly on bottom. Casting minnowbaits from the shelf below the steel seawall, at the northeastern corner of the bridge, around twilight is also productive.

Catfish running from 3 to 15 pounds (cousin Staash calls them miniature Minotaurs), thrive in the deep current, and hit cut bait, Berkley's Catfish Bait Chunks, and shrimp fished on bottom. Sheepshead and bass like the moving water, too, and take crayfish, worms and jigs.

Carp enjoy the caress of deep current, as well. Recreational anglers just looking for "something that pulls back hard," go for them with vegetarian fare like kernel corn, bread balls, and bouillon-size pieces of boiled potato.

And then there are serious carpers like Mike McGrath, owner of Syracuse based McGrath and Associates Carp Angling Services. Having served apprenticeships under Asian and European masters, he's got his technique down to a science.

Mike makes a mash by mixing 6 ounces of Red Bull energy drink with a can of creamed corn (about 15 ounces), and stirring it into 2 pounds of flaked oats (raw oatmeal). Forming a handful of the of the recipe into a patty, he drops a hook baited with a corn puff into the middle, and packs the stuff around it into the size and shape of a hardball. Lobbing it out (you have to ease it out gently; the force of a regular cast will tear the pack apart), he props his rod in a holder, chums the spot with the mash, sits down and waits.

Anywhere from 10 minutes to a half hour later, carp show up and all hell breaks loose. The first thing they run into is the chum scattered around the line baits, and celebrate the find by breaking on the surface. The unlucky ones eat the bait and, feeling the hook pierce their sensitive lips, peel out for the deep, causing the rod to dance in its holder in tune to the reel's tortured drag. When everything goes right, Mike catches hundreds of pounds of these fresh water behemoths—and a few catfish—in a matter of hours.

Some clients hire him just for the cardio-vascular benefits of this type of fishing; others for the excitement of catching trophy-sized fish. Whatever their reason, all agree on one thing: he's worth every penny.

Although the south FAS is harder to get to, the variety of habitats it offers makes the trouble worthwhile. The parking lot off Kathan Road (From I-81 exit 31, Brewerton, head west on Bartel Road, cross the overpass, turn right onto Kathan; the lot is to the right) holds about 50 cars, and offers an asphalt path at its northeastern corner that stretches for a couple of hundred yards to a handicapped-accessible fishing site offering access to the lake and river skirting the highway. Unfortunately, the paved path stops at a bridge over a narrow side-channel, and the rest of the trail along both sides of the I-81 grade—particularly on the river side—is primitive, requiring a degree of effort and agility to negotiate.

The shallow, southern channel and the swampy area on the river side of I-81, offer panfish, pickerel and largemouth bass until early July, when the water reaches unbearable levels and temperatures. However, the slop and weeds thin-out the closer you come to the canal and the holes usually hold fish all summer long. The bass and pickerel respond to wacky-rigged stick-worms tossed into openings in the vegetation, and buzzbaits and spinnerbaits ripped over the weed tops; panfish like worms, minnows and small lures like Beetle Spins, Berkley Atomic Teasers and Honey Worms.

The lakeside is far more popular because a broken line of massive stones, laid flat along the bottom of the grade, makes walking relatively easy. Pickerel, northern pike, largemouth and smallmouth bass, and big panfish thrive in this corner of the lake, and walleyes come up on the shelf near the main channel during the evening. And although the water is shallow and weedy, there's enough of it between the vegetation to make casting relatively problem-free. The whole area is worth fishing in late spring and early summer; and the northern half, where the weeds start thinning out a bit, stays productive all summer long.

James Daher, an employee at North Syracuse's Mickey's Live Bait & Tackle Shop, says top-water lures like Scum Frogs and Snag Proof Boss Rats are popular among anglers he knows who fish the area during local bass tournaments. Cousin Staash considers this one of his favorite spots, and likes twitching Bass Pro's Lazer Eye XPS Minnows early in the morning. The rest of the time he swims worms rigged on spinner harnesses, and jerks Flukes or crankbaits like Live Target Smelt..

The deep channel below the bridge holds smallmouths, walleyes, channel cats, carp and sheepshead. They respond to the same tactics and baits listed for the north FAS above.

41. PERCH TRIANGLE

Jack perch is the local name for large yellow perch. Up until the turn of the century, that meant fish stretching eight inches or better. But "the perch are getting bigger," claims James Daher, an employee of Mickey's Live Bait & Tackle Shop, the oldest bait shop in the Syracuse area. "Nowadays, 12 inchers are expected."

A well rounded angler, James would be hard pressed to put a finger on his favorite species. He's as likely to fish for bass as for walleye, admires northern pike and pickerel, gets animated talking about big catfish, never has anything bad to say about sheepshead, has been known to target carp, and loves panfish. One thing he eagerly admits to is that perch rank high among his favorites.

Thirty years of working the bait shop have taught him a thing or two: "The lake turns over in August. By the end of the month, an algae bloom usually turns the water into pea soup and the perch all but shut down. By mid-September, the bite starts turning around again, slowly at first, accelerating as water temperatures drop. When the water hits the mid-50s, instinct tells the fish to prepare for winter and they go on a feeding binge. My magic formula at this time is: wind, weed edges and 13-foot depth," says the colorful bait monger.

James Daher and a smallie he took vertically fishing a fathead minnow.

James likes to fish with his buddy, David France (he owns the boat), on the lake's west end. James calls the run "the Triangle"; David adds "one of its spots usually produces."

Their first requirement is a breeze. "We won't even go out if it isn't blowing," says James, "preferably out of the north or west, just strong enough to agitate the surface into a ripple or slight chop."

Launching at Oneida Shores County Park, on the South Shore, they head due north. At the channel edge of the weed bed carpeting Big Bay, they search for the magical 13-foot depth. Finding it, they run along the line looking for fish. When they appear, James lowers the anchor.

Attaching enough split-shot to get to bottom, they drop their baits over the side. After touching down, the offerings are raised three to five inches off the floor and still-fished; the only action the worm or minnow get is their natural movements and what the waves dish out.

Dave calls it vertical fishing. "You don't have to cast out because if you're properly positioned at the edge of the weed bed; the perch gather below you to use the boat for cover from the sun."

If a half hour or so goes by without a hit, they move east about two miles to Three Mile Bay. When the hits run out, they move again, this time south, to the weed edges crowning the channel drop off the western tip of Frenchman Island.

James says minnows and worms work equally well for perch, but worms allow you to catch loads of sunfish, too.

"When vertical fishing for perch, use a golden, #6 Aberdeen hook," David advises.

"Oh yeah," David continues, "and be prepared to catch anything that swims in the drink. We always catch huge pickerel and smallmouths, and I've taken several channel cats weighing over 10 pounds," he adds.

42. UP FISH CREEK: LANDLOCKED ATLANTIC SALMON

Fishing on foot might not sound as glamorous as doing it from a souped-up Lund, but it has its benefits. For instance, it's good exercise while moving around looking for hits; and a great way to gather valuable intelligence. That's how word got out about the guy who allegedly caught an Atlantic salmon below the dam in Caughdenoy late in the summer of 2013.

Now, just about anyone who's been fishing the Seneca and Oswego Rivers for any length of time can tell you a story or two about landlocks taken in the whitewater at Oswego, Minetto, Fulton, even Baldwinsville. Experts surmise these fish were stocked by the New York State Department of Environmental Conservation in Lakes Ontario or Cayuga.

But how do you explain an Atlantic salmon in the Oneida River?

The Fish Creek Atlantic Salmon Club, that's how. Formed in 1997, the group has been working to restore the species to its native waters on the eastern half of the Oswego Drainage ever since.

While Fish Creek has never been the primary residence of great numbers of Atlantic salmon, it served as one of Lake Ontario's most important nurseries for the species. In the old days, Lake Ontario claimed the greatest population of landlocked Atlantic salmon in the world until dams, and rampant pollution from industry, all but wiped them out in the beginning of the 19th Century. When it came time to spawn, they ascended all its tributaries, including the Oswego River, its second largest. Formed at the confluence of the Oneida and Seneca Rivers, the Oswego offered the fish access into Oneida Lake and the ideal spawning habitat of its greatest tributary, Fish Creek.

Gene Carey, founding member of the Fish Creek Atlantic Salmon Club, at the hatchery the club built at the McConnellsville Dam on West Branch Fish Creek.

The club's program is funded through dues, raffles, and donations. It raises fry at a hatchery it built on the creek's west branch, at the spillway of Harden Furniture's mill dam in McConnellsville. The company donated the site, as well as a $5,000 grant to build the thing; and Spey Nation has been chipping in with annual grants of $1,500.

According to Eugene Carey, a founding member of the club (he's on the cover of the author's first book *Fishing Eastern New York*), the new facility is working out very well. Its equipment is run by solar power so electrical outages aren't a concern. The creek's fluctuating temperature prepares the fry for the conditions they'll encounter in the wild, and the water's natural nutrients, easily identifiable by the young, spur their appetite so they don't have to be coaxed into feeding by club members.

Incoming reports bear him out. Oneida Lake's ice fishermen have been treated to a smattering of landlocks throughout this century. In the fall of 2011, three beauties ranging from 25 to 27 inches were caught in the canal at Sylvan Beach. In the summer of 2013, two were taken by anglers on the lake.

The dream collectively envisioned by this small, dedicated group of anglers in 1997 is materializing. If the trend continues, Oneida Lake's tributaries will be giving Lake Ontario's feeders serious competition for New York's native salmon.

43. NORTH SHORE'S DEEP SUMMER PERCH

Back in the old days, fishing camps were a staple of Oneida Lake culture. Guys would come up in summer and spend their vacations schmoozing, drinking and fishing. The winds of change stirred by the hippy movement that slowly swept into the second half of the last century revised America's collective consciousness, and the "good ol' boys" began bringing their wives and kids along. The establishments that didn't refurbish their operations to suit family tastes withered on the vine; those that survived turned into resorts and RV parks.

Kirchner's Fishing Camp, on the north shore, chose change. Pete Rich bought the place in 2003 and renamed it Anglers' Bay, a full-service resort offering bait and tackle, cottages, boat rentals, camping and a marina. Rich took to his new occupation with a zest reflecting his youth, making major changes, including converting the former bar and grill into a bait and tackle shop specializing in local brands like Walleye Magnet and Dixie Spinners, items designed specifically for Oneida Lake's walleye and perch.

Boasting a long presence in the area, Rich is an amateur historian. He's got a wealth of anecdotes, including colorful stories of the happy-go-lucky days of the fishing camps, stuff like how the bar doubled as a bed for guests who couldn't make it back to their rooms.

Today, customers keep returning to Anglers' Bay because of its great service and location. Tucked into the side of a hill just east of the Oswego County line, it offers something for everyone, including relief from northerly winds. A weedy, shallow shelf stretches south for a couple of hundred yards, slowly dropping to a depth of 17 feet before leveling off for a few hundred feet, and rising again in a group of parallel humps known as Eaton Shoals. On the southern edge of the formation, the water drops abruptly for 20 feet or so and stays about 40 feet deep just about to the other side.

One of the benefits of staying at a contemporary fishing camp is you get to meet other anglers, like Anthony Ambrosino, a professional photographer who's been coming here every year for the past 32 years. Each of his trips stretches into the dog days of summer, the period, generally in late August, when the lake turns over and resembles pea soup. The bite shuts down so dramatically, most locals simply hang up their fishing poles until autumn.

Tony, on the other hand, goes fishing, scoring enough walleye to keep him coming back—decade after decade. His secret: changing with the conditions.

He likes to flatline crankbaits like XPS Minnows, Reef Runners and Rapala Scatter Raps behind lead core, down to depths of 50 feet. When the water's calm, soupy, and the walleye are uncooperative because they're feeding on booming numbers of gizzard shad or leeches, he responds by cranking up the speed from his normal peak of 1.8 mph, to as much as 2.5 mph. This triggers the walleye's predatory instincts much like a moving string of yarn sets off a cat.

Another adjustment he'll make is drifting instead of anchoring while vertical fishing, explaining: "Sometimes they won't hit a bait that's going up and down. They want it moving away from them."

Back at base camp, Rich offers bait and advice. A skilled angler, he can put you on fish under any conditions.

"Inside Eaton Shoal's buoys, it's great for panfish and smallmouths," he says, adding: "On the outside edge, the drop is good for walleye and smallies. And the deep water beyond that holds perch all summer long."

Walleye anglers have even adopted a chapter from the Finger Lakes angler's playbook: drawing the fish to them by lamp light. Late summer sees a lot of guys anchoring at night in the deep water south of Eaton Shoals (between Godfrey and Chisholm Points), setting up lights to attract gizzard shad, and vertical fishing for the walleyes following them with nightcrawlers and bladebaits up to 20 feet off bottom.

One of Rich's most interesting observations is this: "On this end of the lake, if you like walleye, you love white perch. They give you a clue where the walleyes are. The species has a purple throat, and when a local pro like Mike Domachowske, founder of the Walleye Magnet brand of tackle, catches one, he immediately switches over to a purple-bladed Walleye Magnet spinner-rigged worm harness."

Pete Rowell, Anglers' Bay's general manager adds: "Guys who use blades with hammered finishes do best, especially further in the year."

While we're on the topic of white perch; communicating the whereabouts of walleyes isn't their only benefit. Native, along with the white bass, to the Atlantic Ocean (locals don't generally differentiate between the two, simply calling both silver bass), they're pelagic and inclined to hang out in schools, often near the surface. They hit worms, minnows and small lures violently, fight well for their size and taste great. Get on a school (they can go over a pound) and you can have a ball.

44. CHAPMAN PARK

The pier at Chapman Park in the town of Sullivan ends in about 5 feet of water. Beyond it, the lake's floor continues a fairly steep descent, reaching about 10 feet deep within casting range of the structure. Its close proximity to deep water draws all the popular species, while the fence crowning the platform lures loads of safety-conscious leisure-time anglers, including family groups. Put them together and you get one of the south shore's most popular bottom-fishing sites for anything that swims.

Sunfish, rock bass and small yellow perch thrive around the pier's supports, as well as in the cobbles and weeds along the shoreline. However, they've been stuck a lot since spring, and surviving one or more encounters with man makes them smart—curious enough to investigate a worm thrown their way, but reluctant to hit it without thoroughly examining it first. Still, one of the sunnies or rockies, usually the smallest in the group, will eventually hit a night crawler, especially if it's fat and squirming. On the other hand, they'll all eagerly strike anything new like a jig, tube, or wet fly.

Further out, you'll find open-water species like catfish, sheepshead, small-mouth bass and larger panfish. The smallies and drum are generally targeted with crayfish and worms, but will also hit a 3-inch curly-tail, blade bait or minnowbait. Jumbo catfish come around in the evening and strike gobs of worms, cutbait and shrimp. The panfish hit worms, minnows and small lures.

This is one of the likeliest spots for bank anglers to encounter schools of white perch or white bass. Locals don't usually differentiate between the two, simply calling both silver bass. There is a difference, however: the white perch

Monster Oneida Lake rock bass caught on a rock pile.

have plain, silvery or brown sides, and a purple lower jaw; the white bass come in the same color but have horizontal stripes, much like a striped bass.

Native to the Atlantic Ocean, they're pelagic, usually only coming close to shore to spawn, generally around shoals and islands. Sometimes they'll cruise a bank near deep water. The perch outnumber the bass by 10 to 1; both travel in large schools, often just below the surface. You can tell they're around by all the activity they generate: diving gulls filling the sky, minnows jumping like rising rain.

Normally ranging from 6 to 9 inches, they can reach over 15 inches in years of plentiful food. They're notorious for striking violently, fighting stubbornly, and tasting great. They'll hit worms, minnows and small lures.

Although some walleyes are taken off the pier from June through August, their numbers increase dramatically as summer winds down. By mid-September, they appear so regularly, anglers start seriously targeting them in the evening. In October, the pier becomes one of the lake's most crowded shore-fishing spots for the species.

Mike Kelly, a resident of Camillus, NY, drives 100 miles round-trip, a couple of times a week, to fish here. "The pier can fill up fast," says the former outdoors editor of the Syracuse *Post Standard* and the author of three books. "And even though the best direction to cast is straight out, and the pier offers a nice extension, it can get crowded, but you can still cast out far enough from the bank."

The park is on NY 31, about 1 mile west of Lakeport.

AUTUMN

45. TAKING IT TO THE BANK

September is the best time of year to grab your investment in walleye gear—and pike dreams—and head for the bank.

The sun's annual migration south, a move it starts discreetly in late June, becomes impossible to ignore this month. Setting around 6:30 pm, not rising again until after 7 am, its hang-time in the northern hemisphere is less than half the day, and gets shorter and shorter until late December. Less light means less photosynthesis, translating into fewer weeds, a drop in zooplankton, and cooler temperatures. The resultant food shortage, lack of cover, and cool weather drive bait into shallow water, and walleye follow.

While open-water bait and predators find a degree of comfort around mid-lake shoals, humps, and the shelves skirting the islands, the choicest habitat is found close to shore. Nutrients, relatively moderate temperatures and run-off (murky water that fish find useful for cover) ride the currents of tributaries, and they feed the lake from the bank.

Fish react to changing conditions. One of their greatest motivators is the wind. It stirs up the bottom, especially in shallow water, moving nutrients—and everything that's hungry—towards shore. That's why if you look out over the lake this time of year, even in broad daylight, you won't find many fishing boats out there. They're all in close.

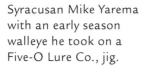

Syracusan Mike Yarema with an early season walleye he took on a Five-O Lure Co., jig.

Dusk contributes to the magic by sweeping away visibility. Emboldened by the decreasing light, fish come in even closer, sometimes into water barely covering their dorsal fins, within easy casting distance of the numerous silhouettes of solitary anglers rising out of the surf in the fading light.

They're not there for bullheads!

Autumn surf-fishing for pike in the evening is about the most exciting way to go for these delicious beasties on Oneida Lake. The setting sun usually puts a damper on the wind, calming down the lake's surface. When the sun's corona creeps below the trees, a twinkling stillness surrounds you, punctuated with splashes of activity.

Schools of gizzard shad invariably swim by. They appear in such numbers, they look like underwater rafts that dimple the surface. Reaching your side, the formation silently splits, wrapping around you like fast-water skirting a rock. Predators attacking from below the school, or its periphery, send showers of silver erupting through the undulating, moonlit glare.

Seeing a walleye hit a minnow within arm's reach is exciting; watching one swim up behind your minnowbait and slam it right in front of you is the greatest.

Walleye withdrawing minnows from the bank will skirt the entire lake from late September until first ice. The best time of day to fish is "the window"

Fall bassin'.

(a half hour each side of sundown), and the most productive period runs from mid-October through mid- November. Good baits are Bass Pro XPS Extreme Minnows, Jr. Thundersticks, Countdown Rapalas and Challenger Minnows.

The lake's entire shoreline hosts magical wading opportunities in fall. A lot of guys try predicting Mr. Walleye's whereabouts according to the wind, fishing the shore it battered all day. However, if you're not inclined to examine meteorological events for clues, live close to a part of the lake that doesn't get much wind, or simply prefer using good ol' intuition, the hotspots below will lead you to fishing satisfaction.

46. SOUTH BAY

This bay's massive weed bed holds a lot of black bass. Both species are present. While it's generally believed smallmouths greatly outnumber largemouths in this end of the lake, tossing a 6-inch wacky-rigged stickworm under boat docks or into nearshore weeds, or running swimbaits over rock piles or deep weeds will generally result in mixed bags.

Mike Yarema says walleye are plentiful around the bay's entrance early in the season, and he gets a lot of them by drifting and casting jigs tipped with pinched crawlers.

The surf behind Marion Manor Marina is a dynamite spot to wade and cast minnowbaits for autumn walleyes. An enterprise of the Oneida Indian Nation, the marina usually allows access to its surf to those who ask, but the facility has been known to refuse permission after anglers have trashed the place. Since there's no policy written in stone, your chances of being granted fishing rights are good just for the asking.

Yarema says South Bay's rock piles are go-to spots for spawning sunfish. There's a big one right behind Oneida Lake Marina.

47. LINEUP AT THE GATEWAY: SYLVAN BEACH

Fish are naturally drawn to current. The reasons vary with the seasons. Spring flows, spurred by snowmelt, guide them to spawning sites. Powered by tributaries, summer currents offer the cool caress of spring-fed feeder streams. Come fall, when water temperatures are dropping, tributaries inject warmer temperatures they carry off the land.

Fish Creek, Oneida Lake's largest tributary, packs the biggest current around.

Driven by its steep slide down the Tug Hill Plateau, the stream pours into the Erie Canal and pushes west, through Sylvan Beach, into Oneida Lake.

Penetrating deep into the drink, its plume draws massive quantities of the lake's nomadic species into the waterway's clear, relatively comfortable flow, within easy reach of anglers casting under the resort hamlet's neon.

Without a doubt, Sylvan Beach is Oneida Lake's most popular fishing destination. Two concrete walls, each about 0.25 mile long, line both sides of the Erie Canal's last leg, offering convenient fishing platforms, complete with benches, trash cans, and waterfront parking.

For the most part, folks fishing the lake's gateway in autumn have walleye on their minds. They use every technique in the book, from slowly walking the wall while dragging minnows or worms, to standing in place and vertically working Rapala Jigging Raps, snap-jigging XPS Lazer Blades, jerking suspending XPS Extreme Minnows, and twitching or swimming floating crankbaits.

But they're not the only ones. This section of the canal also draws sedentary temperaments looking for quality still-fishing opportunities. They set their sights on a steady stream of popular species that moves through constantly in search of comfortable winter quarters: monster sheepshead, trophy channel catfish and panfish the size of frying-pans.

The catfish—and an occasional sturgeon—hit cutbait, minnows and shrimp; sheepshead and smallies have a taste for crayfish; and everything takes night crawlers.

There's always panfish to keep you busy when the walleye aren't biting.

The canal's north wall ends in a breakwater—canal on the south side, lake to the north. Anglers have access to about 100 feet of it before running into a chain-link gate bearing a no-trespassing sign—even calm days see rogue waves slam into the wall with enough force to knock a big man into the water. The jetty continues for a few more yards before ending in the broken, decaying remains of the original, 1000-foot-long barrier bearing a light at its end.

The south wall isn't as long. Starting below the NY 13 bridge, it ends in a beach a couple of hundred yards short of the lake. A sand bar just off shore offers dynamite surf-fishing at the mouth of the canal. And while its floor is smooth, offering relatively solid footing, waterlogged windfalls divert the current in a couple of spots, allowing it to sweep out large holes that can swamp the boots of careless waders.

Regardless of what side of the canal you're on, the sunsets are spectacular. Still, the view from the south bank is unusual . . . even scary. At the point, sand bars reach to just a hair below the surface, creating an effect akin to bald spots in the waves. Massive root balls crown the shallow shelf. Their spooky tentacles reach out of the water like drowning fingers grasping for air, while the sun dances through the tangled mass in a burst of burning embers.

Back on the Sylvan Beach side, the atmosphere is civilized, even festive. Neon from waterfront restaurants like the Canal View and the Crazy Clam illuminates the night, while their throbbing music makes it rock. Out front, anglers walk the wall bobble-headed, jigging their lures to the beat.

48. GODFREY POINT'S SOUND GARDEN

Godfrey Point juts out of the north shore like an old tooth. The NYSDEC boat launch at the dent in its crown is accessible through a narrow channel marked by pencil buoys. The waterfront lining the rest of the property is so shallow, canoes scrape bottom before making it to the beach.

Shallow water so close to the deepest part of the drink is the spot's greatest draw. Muddy and pebbly, its bottom is friendly to weed growth and vegetation starts popping up right at the edge of the gently sloping stonework shoring up the bank. At the end of September, when the rest of the lake's public access areas start sprouting the season's first surf anglers in the twilight, the weeds of Godfrey Point are still so thick—so eager to corrupt every cast—anglers with common sense stay away until about mid-October, after early birds like this author have cut the tops of the weeds with our casts, and what remains lies down for the winter.

So what draws a small following of loners to this spot's aggravating vegetation at summer's end? Walleyes, that's what!

They storm the surf in the wakes of massive schools of gizzard shad that move in to take advantage of comfortable temperatures stirred into the shallows by the season's shorter days and cooler nights. Like everything else in this sport, however, there's no fool-proof formula for predicting exactly when the evening atmosphere will start taking more heat out of the water than the sun can replace. One thing's for certain, though, it'll start in stages.

For instance, the bait's first reconnaissance run to the bank might be spurred by a hard August rain. The next may be spurred by an early September cold front. By the end of the month, gizzard shad can appear inshore twice a week, jumping to four times a week by mid-October. Afterward, you can expect rafts of minnows in the shallows every evening up to the week before Thanksgiving.

But some guys can't wait for that schedule to come around. Knowing that nature loves uncertainty and doesn't like man-made timetables, they look for clues to early opportunities the old way; studying the mist and using their intuition.

"When the steam comes off the lake at night, we lose three degrees the next morning," claims Pete Rich, owner of Anglers' Bay, a fishing resort off NY 49, a short distance east of Godfrey Point.

And that happens in September more often than a lot of anglers think. A three-day cold spell knocking temperatures down by 10 degrees is enough to spur bait into the relative safety of the shallows for a night or two, until temperatures rise again.

The nicest thing about fishing Godfrey Point at dusk this time of year is the pleasant weather. September's evening temperatures, though much cooler than August's, are still relatively mild. As a rule, the difference in the thermometer between day and night isn't too extreme yet, so the wind doesn't go into its rabid, pre-winter mode. Even if the air is stirred up by a cold front, southwesterly or southeasterly winds, the fishing access site's location on the point's east bank, at the bottom of a shallow, wooded hill, offers a degree of protection, making it comfortable enough oftentimes to fish in short sleeves.

If you hit it just right, you'll feel stillness sweep over the countryside as the last traces of orange drop below the western sky. The evening's quiet irons the waves out of the water, leaving its surface ranging from gently undulating to mirror-like. Before long, rafts of gizzard shad spread over the surface. Emboldened by the dark, walleye follow the bait into shore. Bent on a feeding binge, they come in so close, and in such numbers, the sucking, slurping, and splashing sounds of their foraging send a spooky symphony over the waterscape.

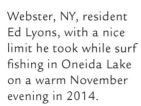

Webster, NY, resident Ed Lyons, with a nice limit he took while surf fishing in Oneida Lake on a warm November evening in 2014.

Godfrey Point's sound garden offers the lake's most sensuous fishing, often steeped in solitude. And being alone, able to cast wherever your heart desires, adds frosting to this spot's appeal. You see, while September's evening song is music to just about every angler's ears, most don't have the time and patience to indulge it. The tenacious weed bed out front endlessly grabbing your hooks is enough to wear down the most patient amongst us. Indeed, many find a September fishing trip to this place quickly deteriorates along these lines:

1st cast: A shake of the head in disgust.
2nd: Mild curse.
3rd: Harsher curse.
4th: Using the Lord's name in vain.
5th: Smacking the lure on the water with such force you send a minor tsunami slamming into shore.
6th: Slapping the lure against the waves so hard, everyone in the neighborhood runs outside to see the source of the explosion.
7th: Pulling handfuls of hair out of your head.
8th: Scratching your new bald spots while deciding your next move.
9th: Packing up and heading for Sylvan Beach or Cleveland Dock.

But it doesn't have to be this way. By exercising a little patience, you not only stand a good chance of pulling a walleye out of the salad, you'll also have exciting memories for years to come.

Just play the splash. In other words, when you hear or see (the launch has lights) a walleye breaking surface after a minnow, cast a floating crankbait like a Bass Pro XPS Lazer Eye towards it; you don't have to hit right on top of it, just near it. A bait-ball's survival depends on its individual members working in unison to confuse its prey, so walleye don't always hit their target. And even if they do, they're on a feeding binge and can stack two or three shad in their gullets at once. If you can cast your bait into the widening ring formed by a takedown, there's a good chance the excited fish, or one next to it (pike seldom travel alone) will hit.

Don't retrieve the bait, just let it sit for a count to 10, twitch it and let it sit some more. If nothing hits after a few seconds, twitch it again. Still nothing; give it another twitch. You should be able to get two to three twitches before weeds foul the hooks. In the meantime, brace yourself for a hit from a walleye, too.

Twitching for walleye requires patience and imagination. But it's worth it. The hit is invariably violent and the splash breathtaking.

When autumn solidly paints the background, and the weeds thin out or lay down, taking walleyes from the bank is about as easy as it gets. In fact, they come in so heavy at times, that even under the harshest fall conditions—what locals call extreme fishing—you'll be able to see and hear them through the whitecaps slapping the shoreline. At times like this, you can cast anywhere there's water, and you're likely to catch a limit.

Unlike most of the other surf-fishing hotspots around the lake, you don't need to wade out up to your waist at Godfrey Point. In fact you don't need to wade at all, the fish come right to shore; you can see them parting the grass and the light in their eyes.

49. CLEVELAND DOCK SHUFFLE

Oneida Lake has been splitting the state in half for as long as anyone can remember. Anything above it is considered "up north," points south are just New York. The northerners love their walleyes, and never let a good one go—unless they've already caught their limit . . . and somebody's watching (even then, they'll usually offer their extra fish to the guy standing next to them). Come autumn, one spot that gets the lion's share of these good ol' boys is the NYSDEC's Cleveland Dock Fishing Access Site.

Black Creek slices through the north shore village of Cleveland's east end. It pours a lot of water into Wells Bay, creating a plume that reaches out into the lake, hooking massive schools of gizzard shad with the promise of soothing temperatures at its mouth. And as any walleye lover worth his weight in jig-heads can tell you, where you find massive quantities of these little beasties, you'll find walleyes.

Over the millennia, Black Creek has built a point, cutting a relatively deep channel along its east bank. In the 18th century, a time when Cleveland was putting itself on the map with industries ranging from glass and boat manu-facturing to logging and tanning, a harbor was built, complete with a long, concrete dock along the deep edge, and breakwaters to protect the entrance.

By the early years of the 20th century, industry disappeared from the vil-lage, but the dock from which horse-drawn wagons loaded ships remains. The state built a fishing access site on it, and it's become one of the most popular bank-fishing spots on the lake.

Although the dock's deep water attracts sheepshead, channel catfish, and panfish year-round, locals up here boast they have good taste, and mostly fish the place in autumn, when loads of walleye come around.

The fish don't find the whole place to their liking, however. In fact, you'll seldom find actively feeding fish this time of year at the entrance to Wells Bay, or in the deep water off the dock. They're chasing shad that are on the surface; bait that's drawn to the area by the mouth of Black Creek and the relative safety of the shallow water running the shoreline east of it.

So the most valuable fishing spot is the 10 yards or so at the seawall's northern tip. The angler standing at the end can cast into the marina's en-trance and along the north bank. The two or three people standing south of him are in good positions to cast east, and run their lures along the shallow north shore, too; often getting the first shot at walleyes moving into the area from the southeast. Those standing further south have a chance of nailing suspended walleye entering the bay along the wall, but they're few.

When pike are in, they can be so thick, that on calm nights—when there's no wave action, mind you—their noisy foraging on the surface sounds like white caps crashing on shore. During these times there's enough walleye to go around, and anglers take their positions in what looks like a one-sided line dance cousin Staash calls the "Cleveland Dock Shuffle."

The smart ones, and those that have time on their hands, ensure they get the sweet spots by arriving early. The bite generally doesn't start smoking until around sundown, and then all hell can break loose. The first to get their limits are the guys closest to the end. When they leave, the dudes standing next in line move in. And while the last guy must feel like it's taking forever to get up front, when he finally does, he stands a chance of limiting out, too.

Under the right conditions, it only takes about an hour for a lineup of six to eight guys to get their limits. Granted, this kind of action doesn't happen all the time; just enough to draw grown men to Cleveland Dock to dance.

View of Cleveland Dock from NY 49.

50. CLEVELAND'S BREAK WATERS

Not everyone can get out of their daily responsibilities early enough to claim a choice slot on the wall at the NYSDEC's Cleveland Dock Fishing Access Site during autumn's walleye bite. Some, their day sabotaged by daylight savings time, arrive after dark and can't see endlessly casting into what they consider empty water along the sea wall while waiting their turn at its head. For them, the dock offers another option, its breakwaters.

Back in the day when Cleveland's industries made it one of the north shore's economic powers, two barriers blocked Oneida Lake's whitecaps from sweeping into the harbor at full force. Ice from many winters has taken its toll on the structures, tearing them apart and knocking huge sections off their foundations.

Reaching out into the lake from the southern tip of the CDFAS, the west wall takes the full force of spring's assault on winter. As the lake's icy cloak breaks up, the wind and waves drive the massive floes against the structure. Ramming it, piling up, constantly shifting, the jagged chunks grind and gouge what remains, giving silent testimony to the violence of ice-out. The original form still reaches out from the bank, but when it reaches the water, it breaks up, its pieces scattered by the elements. The fish don't mind; indeed, they find the debris ideal cover for ambush.

Gizzard shad, and the train of walleyes constantly at their backs, access the harbor from the west by swimming over the ruins. A good place to head them off is in the surf east of the decaying wall (the breakwater is on posted land). Cast minnowbaits parallel to the structure for walleyes cruising the north shore's minnow-rich shallows; east for fish coming in or going out of Cleveland Dock.

Sitting in relatively deep water out in Wells Bay, the eastern breakwall is spared much of the violence that ice-out visits on its counterpart. And though it appears as a shoal to the naked eye standing at the dock, when you get up close and personal, its original form—rounded surfaces and all—is still well defined.

The only way to reach the eastern breakwall is by boat. But it's well worth it because a lot of fish come into Cleveland Dock from that side. In addition, the habitats surrounding it, including relatively deep water on its south and west sides, and the weed edges and breaks along the north shore, always hold walleye, smallies and yellow perch. What's more, autumn's roving schools of gizzard shad and walleyes reach this spot up to an hour before they make it to the dock, offering day anglers good shots at filling their limits while it's still light out.

Ohio native Don Ludwig holding a nice bronzeback he took on a darter at Cleveland, NY's, east Break wall.

In the afternoon, these fish will take suspending Bass Pro XPS Lazer Eye minnows that are swimmed or worked like a jerkbait, jigged bladebaits, and worms on spinner harnesses dragged slowly on bottom. As it gets darker, bring your baits closer to shore and the surface.

The NYSDEC boat launch at Godfrey Point is less than two miles east, so getting here is fairly easy.

51. PHILLIPS POINT TWILIGHT SERENADE

Sprawling over almost 3500 acres of forest and marsh, Three Mile Bay Wildlife Management Area is the largest parcel of undeveloped land on the lake, and three miles of it hugs the north shore. Unlike state forests, which are designed to provide wood products and subject to harvest, WMAs are run to enhance wildlife habitat and must remain pristine by law. The authorities in charge of the place take this rule so seriously, they don't maintain the last mile of McCloud Road (off Toad Harbor Road), and let its ruts get deeper and deeper, discouraging all but the most serious outdoor lovers.

And they keep coming, year after year. Some to admire the towering old growth maples, and other hardwoods lining the road, their crowns so high you can't identify their leaves with the naked eye. Others to see the awesome screen their foliage paints on the autumn sky. A few make the bouncy journey to launch kayaks and canoes from the landing at the tip of Phillips Point. The vast majority, however, comes to surf-fish, steeped in the magical sounds of the point's twilight serenade.

Night woods are very active, especially near water. Standing in the lake up to your privates, waving a long rod to cast your dreams for walleye dinners, doesn't make a lot of noise; not enough to stop animals on shore from coming down for a drink, anyway. They slowly make their way down the hill toward you, rustling the leaves, communicating with grunts and other vocalizations, including howling. Indeed, Cousin Staash believes the major reason walleye congregate so heavily off the point is "to watch the dancing silhouettes the critters cast against moonlit stretches of the beach." (Uncle John claims Staash's mom used to discipline the boy as a child by dropping him on his head; Aunt Matilda argues her husband was the culprit; Staash can't remember.)

But that's neither here nor there. What matters is that decent numbers of walleye, along with a smattering of pickerel, perch and smallies are always present because schools of gizzard shad bottleneck while rounding the point. Savvy locals wade out into the surf directly in front of the point's tip and cast minnowbaits.

Get there from Central Square (I–81 exit 32) by heading east on NY 49 for 3 miles, turning right onto Toad Harbor Road, then left about 3 miles later onto McCloud Drive and traveling 1 mile to the end.

52. EXIT STRATEGY: I-81

Cousin Staash considers autumn's surf-bite the walleye's gift to local fishermen.

"The pikes' forays to the bank each evening coincide with quitting time, giving everyman the chance to load up his freezer for winter," he says. "Take me, for instance, I work until 3:30. It takes me a half hour to get to Brewerton; 10 minutes to unload and get to the water. That leaves me the evening window to fish for walleye in the surf."

His favorite spot this time of year is the NYSDEC public fishing access site at the north end of the I-81 bridge. Not only because it's convenient, but because it lets him take advantage of what he calls the "exit strategy."

According to his theory, "The bottleneck at the source of the Oneida River draws two distinct populations of walleyes, lake- and river-run, doubling my chances of scoring."

Consisting of schools of 2- to 3-year-olds, ranging from too short to about 19 inches, many of the lake-run fish are originally from the west side of the

Bass pros working the shelf along the eastern shoulder of I-81.

lake, but head for the comfort of the deeper, darker waters on the other end when things start to heat up in July. Just as they're getting spoiled in the dark depths, pigging out on the massive schools of minnows luxuriating in the open water's rich food supplies, autumn pulls the plug with its double whammy of shorter days and cooler water temperatures. The food supply now not what it used to be, the schools begin heading west again to ease their hunger pangs.

Autumn takes a similar toll on the easy pickings of river fish. Accustomed to feeding in current, they naturally follow the flow, eventually ending up at the lake's outlet.

Both populations hang out in the deep water by day, and hit deep-running crankbaits, bladebaits and live bait fished on bottom.

In the evening, schools of gizzard shad and buckeyes, emboldened by the fading light's deteriorating visibility, invade the shallows to take advantage of the warmer temperatures planted there by daylight. Walleyes follow hot on their tails.

The iron seawall along the shelf on the northeastern corner of the bridge stops the bait in its tracks. Walleye corral the minnows, pinning them against the corrugated iron, and charge in one at a time to pick them off.

This is a local hotspot among the surf-fishing crowd. Work floating lures like Bass Pro's XPS Extreme Minnows and Rapalas between the channel drop and the seawall. Vary your retrieve. Hitting the metal with the lure every now and then sounds the dinner bell. Cast tight to the bridge abutment periodically, and twitch and swim the lure along the concrete.

But there's another side to this story: the FAS on the other end of the bridge. Requiring a walk of several hundred yards to get to the water, it's not as popular as the northern site—during the week, anyway. On weekends, however, when you have a little more time, the spot's numerous habitats can be very rewarding.

The grade anchoring on this side of the bridge stretches for several hundred yards. The shallow shelf on both sides draws hungry bass, pickerel, northerns, and panfish looking to fatten up for winter. They'll take buzzbaits, spinnerbaits, and live bait all day long.

And then you have the deep water in the main channel. During daylight, fat-bodied crankbaits retrieved at a slow clip, and Texas-rigged 7-inch worms, jigged gently or dragged slowly on bottom, up the drop-off, will result in some nice bronzebacks and bucketmouths; while bucktails and deep-diving crankbaits, worked in the channel and along its drop, will generally attract a walleye or two.

Walleye taken at the I-81 North Fishing Access Site in Brewerton.

At night, smallies and walleyes come up on the lakeside shelf and hit swim-baits and minnowbaits. On the riverside, largemouths move in close to shore and can't seem to keep their mouths shut whenever a noisy popper, buzzbait or prop bait swims by and throws bubbles in their faces.

53. SCRAMBLING AND WADING AT ONEIDA SHORES

Occupying roughly half of Muskrat Bay, Oneida Shores County Park offers the longest stretch of public wading access on the south shore. And while the entire bay draws every predatory species in the lake to its minnow-rich shallows in autumn, its most productive spot allows you to cast crankbaits from the middle of October until first ice blocks your shots, without ever having to get your feet wet.

"The rock jetty off the boat launch is a local hot spot for walleye in the fall," claims Al Daher, of Mickey's Live Bait and Tackle Shop in North Syracuse. "Why wade if you don't have to?" he asks, with a shrug.

Some would argue that the difficulty of maintaining your balance on the point's massive chunks of cut limestone is why.

To which he replies: "You just gotta be careful."

Bass boat off the launch break wall at Oneida Shores County Park. The jetty is a popular platform for casting crankbaits for autumn walleye.

And he's right. Although the boulders sit helter-skelter, they've settled nicely over the years and there's nothing shaky about them. You'll have to scramble to get out on them, but the top of the structure's spine is high enough off the water to stay dry even at the windiest of times, allowing a steady angler wearing rubber soles to easily move from rock to rock, and even find flat spots to cast from.

It's well worth the trouble, too. Muskrat Bay only averages about 3 feet deep. The jetty extends the natural point, to within casting distance of water that's anywhere from 6 inches to a couple of feet deeper, into a natural staging area that draws bait and walleyes up to a half hour earlier than the surrounding shallows. They mill around for a while, waiting for sunset to pull the shade down over the lake before moving further into shore.

Still, getting your feet wet by wading off the point offers its own excitement. Sometime in mid-autumn, inshore temperatures drop to levels that all of the lake's denizens find comfortable. Panfish come in close to feed on all the life hiding out in the pebbles, rock fields, weeds and reeds. While generally not the size of the hawgs occupying the deep water a few hundred yards off shore, schools of yellow perch up to 10 inches long swarm into the pebbly shallows, joining the spot's year-round, 6- to 8-inch residents. They're especially fun to catch along the edges of reed stubble crowning humps and lining the shore. They hit worms, minnows and small swimbaits like the Berkley 2-inch Ripple Shad.

Black Bass and pickerel share the edges of emergent vegetation with them, but are also plentiful over rocks and weeds further out in the bay. A fun way to get them in broad daylight is to dress in camouflage and slowly, silently wade the shoreline while casting spinnerbaits and buzzbaits. Foraging in water barely covering their backs, and possessed with a deep sense of urgency to fatten up before the snow, they hit with such extreme violence that they often catapult through the surface in explosions of spray and foam.

Come evening, switch over to a floating minnowbait and cast straight out for walleye.

Wading in the park is about as convenient as it gets. The launch has a huge parking lot and a campground occupies the point; its manicured grounds make access to the water easy.

54. JOSEPH F. WILLIAMS MEMORIAL PARK

This Town of Cicero park sits on a tiny point jutting out of the relatively straight shoreline running between Norcross (east end of Lower South Bay) and Hitchcock (mouth of Chittenango Creek) Points. It's straddled by a shallow sandy beach to the east, and a gently sloping shelf to the west. The dumping grounds due north, and Chimney Bar a little ways east, pump a steady stream of walleye and smallmouth to within casting distance of the park on autumn evenings.

Located right where the water meets Lakeshore Road (0.5 mile east of its intersection with Cicero Center Road), its parking lot and easy beach access make the park a favorite spot for anglers wanting to take advantage of the lake's autumn surf bite but don't have a lot of time to do it. They can pretty much cover the area during the window, a half-hour on either side of sunset.

Walleye start showing up as early as September, soon after the swimming season ends. However, the best numbers come around in October and November. They hit all the popular minnowbaits.

A lot of walleye also come to shore west of the swimming beach in the early weeks of the season. Unfortunately, spring fish tend to be school-size, the kind you have to measure to make sure they're big enough to keep.

The park offers a floating dock on its west end from May to October. It's a good platform for casting for black bass during periods of low boat traffic. They'll hit top water lures when the lake's surface is calm, and spinnerbaits any time.

Come winter, the park offers the closest, free public access to Dunham and Frenchman Islands, and even has a snowmobile path to the lake's edge.

Although the park closes at sundown, anglers can get a permit to fish after dark from the Town of Cicero Parks Department (315-699-5233).

55. LARKIN POINT

One of the most productive spots to wade for autumn walleye is the surf at Oneida Lake Beach Association. Stretching from Larkin Point to Syracuse Herald Avenue, a distance of roughly 0.5 mile, its relatively gentle slope takes several hundred yards to drop to 30-feet deep before leveling off. Along the way, its mix of boulders, rock piles and weeds offers ideal cover and forage for decent numbers of the lake's predators year-round.

From mid-September through first ice, however, the shallows within a couple of hundred yards of shore load up with massive quantities of walleye, small schools of perch, and a smattering of smallies. They gather here around nightfall, especially when the wind disturbs the surface—indeed, the harder the blow, the better—to feed on gizzard shad.

The bait is drawn to this magical section of the south shore by the prevailing northwest wind. Not only for the food it carries across the widest part of the lake, but also for the stained water and cornucopia pumped into the drink by Canaseraga Creek. The stream's plume runs north on a relatively easy course protected by Lake Port Bay's west bank. At Gifford Point, however, it enters open water and is at the mercy of the elements. Its cover gone, the northwest wind slams into it, forcing the current to bank hard to the right and push east along the Association's waterfront.

This effect is so reliable, that on any windy night, you'll find up to 20 guys in the surf. When the action really heats up, they turn their headlamps on so frequently to land and stringer fish, they create a light show. (Rumor has it that visiting motorists feasting their senses on the area's spectacular sunsets have mistaken the lights, especially green ones, for UFOs and other extraterrestrials, spawning stories of flashing Nessies or twinkling Martians prowling Lakeport Bay's shoreline at night.)

Walleye don't always come easy. They're notorious for hitting under hurricane winds, exacting a toll in discomfort for every one you catch. Around here they call it extreme fishing: standing waist-high in whitecaps, putting up with waves slamming into your groin, chest and face—while you happily crank all the popular plugs. On a good night, a competent angler can catch his limit in a half hour or less.

Your average angler wouldn't even consider fishing under these conditions. And the typical surfer out here understands, counts his blessings and keeps stringering walleye, grateful that extreme hardship creates memorable moments.

For instance, imagine the wind blowing in your face so hard you can only cast 20 feet. The water rises to your chest and drops to shin-level. The lure is almost at your ankles and a walleye hits it in the trough barely covering your toes.

Or how about watching a swell come in and trying to reel so your line stays in it. As it approaches, the shallows force it into a whitecap. While watching your lure swimming in the wall below the curl, you see an open-mouthed walleye suddenly appear and inhale it. You set the hook and the fish shoots out of the wave.

"You just don't see stuff like that on calm days," cousin Staash explains to justify his love for fishing wind-ravaged surf.

But there's a large thorn in paradise: the beach is restricted to Association members and their guests. Early on, the unwashed masses try sneaking in among the lineup, but their cars give them away. A couple of calls to the county sheriff by irate property owners is all it normally takes to discourage party crashers. They don't get busted for parking—you can park your car on any shoulder that doesn't have a sign warning motorists against it—they get nailed for trespassing on private property while in route to and from the lake.

Jake Maxwell, Lakeport, NY, landing a walleye he took in his backyard, just east of Larkin Point.

Since no one owns the rain, coming in by water is OK. In fact, local guides sometimes anchor 50 to 100 yards off shore, often right in the middle of surf-anglers. What's more, if you're lucky enough to hit the area on a weeknight when there aren't too many guys out there, you can drift and cast, and that's about the surest way to find a limit.

Walleye and smallies chasing gizzard shad in the twilight bravely and boldly go wherever they want to, provided there's at least a foot of water or so. If you should find yourself wondering where to cast, solve the conundrum by throwing anywhere there's water.

There's no deep trough beyond Larkin Point so you needn't worry about falling off the deep end. Still, its boulders are stealthy, its rock beds unstable and slippery, so walk cautiously.

56. LEWIS POINT

One of the lake's most prominent landmarks—and the only meaningful one on the eastern half—Lewis Point is an oasis on this structure-starved end. Its close proximity to deep water draws walleye year-round.

They hit all the usual suspects, but are especially partial to worms. It doesn't matter how you fish them, drifted on bottom with three-way swivel-rigged worm harnesses, tipped on bucktail jigs and worked on the drop-off,

Burt Menninger, Lakeport, NY, gets another.

deep trolled on weight-forward spinners or slow death rigs; as long as there's a worm involved, they'll hit.

Keep an eye peeled for schools of walleye near the surface. A good way to get these fish is to keep a spare rod handy loaded with a worm on a weightless harness, or even a floating jighead, and fire it at the school whenever one shows up on the graph. In many cases you'll be disappointed to catch white bass or white perch, but don't be because they fight well and taste great, too.

In June and July, walleye suspend over the drop-off running from Messenger Bar (1 mile west) to just east of the point. They can be taken by flatlining Deep Thundersticks or Wally Divers, or dragging floating minnowbaits like Smithwick Rogues and Live Target Smelt behind lead core, 16 to 24 feet deep.

The walleye surf bite is the point's greatest attraction in autumn. On most nights from mid-October to the first week of December, anglers wade onto the bar on the point's northeastern corner and cast floating minnowbaits.

Owned by McCraith Beverages, Inc., of New York Mills, near Utica, the shoreline is closed to the general public in summer. But the firm allows the public to fish on the property from October 15 through April 1. Park in the lot off to the right at the end of Lewis Point Road and follow the signs onto the property.

WINTER

SOME CLAIM ICE-FISHING is Central New York's fastest growing sport. Statistics showing retail giant Gander Mountain's Cicero store sells more ice-fishing equipment than any other retailer in the entire Northeast supports their argument. And while dropping a maggot into a hole in the ice and pulling out a fish is magical, it's also dangerous. The New York State Department of Environmental Conservation's website offers an informative feature on ice-fishing, covering everything from clothing to tackle and techniques. Check it out at www.dec.ny.gov/outdoor/7733.html.

If you're new to the sport and don't have time to read the above article, the most important thing you should know is the strength of ice. Below is a short list of DEC's recommendations:

ICE THICKNESS	PERMISSIBLE LOAD
2 inches	one person on foot
3 inches	group in single file
7.5 inches	one car
10 inches	light truck (2.5 tons)

Another good thing to remember is to stay clear of tributary mouths, even if they're frozen over.

57. BIG BAY ON ICE

Most ice-fishing stories set on Oneida Lake cover its fantastic walleye and perch fishing. And that's only right, seeing how these two tasty species thrive in just about every gallon of the lake

But there's more under the hardwater than just these two; namely, sunfish and crappie, two of the most sought after species in the state. And while they're usually thought of as summer game, they're very active in winter, too, especially on sunny days.

And the best spot on the lake to get them is Big Bay, that big dent in the lake's northwestern corner with woods all around it. Averaging 8 feet deep, loaded with weeds, it's the perfect habitat for these sumptuous critters.

What's more, ice on the bay comes early, thickens quickly and stays late, come hell or high water. Indeed, even during winter thaws, when the majority of anglers stay home or close to shore, guys swarm all over Big Bay.

Sunnies, primarily bluegills, run anywhere from 4-inch runts to the size of a big man's hand. They're inclined to strike tiny fare like ice dots tipped with mousies and spikes. Crappies running from 9 to 13 inches will hit the same baits but prefer larger offerings like hardware tipped with waxworms or fish dinners (buckeyes and fathead minnows).

If you're going to be targeting calicoes with minnows, be prepared to tackle with some pickerel. While they're despised by shallow thinkers who hate them because they fear their sharp teeth, they're admired by environmentally savvy anglers who appreciate the dent they're putting in the lake's exploding populations of exotics ranging from alewives to round gobies. In addition, they're popular among connoisseurs who target them for their sweet taste.

Crappies and sunfish move around a lot throughout the water column, and are as likely to strike right below the ice as over the heads of weeds, or on bottom along the edges of vegetation, so fish at various depths until you find them.

Big Bay's west bank is heavily developed with private residences and shoulder parking is prohibited from December 1 through April 1. While some guys ignore the rules and take their chances with getting a parking ticket, you can play it safe by parking in Big Bay Marina at the end of Camic Road (off CR 37, north side of Brewerton) or the self-storage facility's lot at the juncture of Kellar Road/Kellar Spur, for a fee. If you chose the latter, get to the lake by walking Kellar Spur to the end and taking the right-of-way between the two houses.

The northeastern shore traces the NYSDEC's Three Mile Bay/Big Bay Wildlife Management Area and is accessible from the Toad Harbor Fishing Access Site off Shaw Road (from NY 49, head south on Toad Harbor Road for a little over 3 miles, turn right on Shaw Road and continue for about 0.5 mile); unfortunately, this site isn't always plowed.

58. HARDWATER VILLAGE AT SYLVAN BEACH

Halloween is Sylvan Beach's last hurrah for the year. After staging its "Blood Bath," the lights go out on the amusement park and the whole village slips into quiet mode. Anglers continue targeting walleye by casting minnowbaits from the surf, and by walking the canal walls dragging minnows or vertically working Jigging Raps. But they're like autumn leaves; slowly, steadily blowing away, disappearing altogether by ice time.

The village doesn't have to wait until spring for sprouts of visitors to re-emerge, however. A couple nights of freezing temperatures are all it takes to turn the surface of the water on the west bank into the icy platform that'll transform the sleepy hamlet into the most popular ice-fishing spot in Central New York.

The lake's hard complexion doesn't come easily. December winds do their best to prevent winter from paving the place. Swooping down from the north most mornings, they tear into the ice that formed the night before, piling it into sparkling shards on shore and leaving them at the mercy of the late autumn sun.

By the end of the month, however, the lake's shallowness works against it. Warm temperatures rise through the water column, escaping in the mist you see shrouding the lake on cold autumn mornings. The season's last sunny days can't replace it, and what little heat remains is forced to the surface where it's caught by the waves and tossed into the air. By year's end, water temperatures drop to between 32 and 34 degrees Fahrenheit, and the law governing hot and cold is suddenly stood on its head: the warmer water sinks to bottom and the cold layer rises to the top.

A few more days of below-freezing temperatures and the wind switches sides. Charging savagely over the waterscape, it generates whitecaps up to three feet high. The wave tips explode into myriads of tiny ice formations. Crashing to shore, they gain toeholds up and down the beach, building a crust of ice around the lake. Each succeeding wave piles additional slivers of ice onto the ring, welding them in place with frozen foam. A silent night later, a twinkling skim blankets the surface, and a few wintry days after that, ice grips the lake in its frozen embrace for the season.

It only takes about a week of winter conditions for the lake's surface to turn into safe ice. On the first day, only those hopelessly hooked on ice-fishing test the hard water. When they come back and rave about it, the news spreads fast and by the following Saturday, a colorful village of shanties springs up on the ice off Sylvan Beach.

On weekends when the sky is squeaky clean and blue—even if temperatures are in the teens—there's more activity on the lake than there is on Labor Day. Numerous ice-fishing shelters add splashes of brilliant colors over the winter waterscape; the frosty air is filled with the conversations of their tenants, and play-by-play action of basketball and football games. Snowmobiles and ATVs dart back and forth like ice lizards, dodging countless man-drawn sleds creeping across the ice and snow.

And everywhere in between, lone anglers sit out in the open on five-gallon buckets, over water ranging from 15 to 25 feet deep. Often surrounding themselves with tip-ups loaded with buckeyes or fathead minnows, they sit over a hole targeting walleye and large perch by gently shaking hardware like Swedish Pimples tipped with minnows or perch eyes. Others use tiny ice jigs tipped with small minnows or insect larvae for perch (white and yellow).

The ice is generally thick enough to support all this activity by the first of the year; oftentimes even before Christmas.

And while the action isn't generally so hot you'll worry about the ice melting in congested areas, as often as not it's exciting enough to keep the cold at bay. Asked how they were biting one cold, winter day not long ago, a local woman answered "they ain't exactly jumping out of the holes to get in my bucket; but they're biting steady, just enough to keep the excitement flowing and put dinner on the table tonight."

Back on the beach, the village offers ample parking, including a massive lot behind the amusement park which offers easy access to fairly deep water, and has a public toilet. If you don't mind traveling up to a half mile to get to deep water, free parking with access is available on Lakeshore Road, on the north side of town.

59. VIENNA BAR: GRAND SLAM CAPITOL OF ONEIDA LAKE

Although it may sound like a popular watering hole, the Vienna Bar doesn't offer beverages. Nor does it have flat-screened TVs, so don't go expecting to see basketball games either. What you can expect, however, is a different kind of high, the rush that comes with an Oneida Lake Grand Slam: pulling a limit of walleye through the ice, followed by a limit of perch.

Both species love the place. Craig Storms, head of Stormy Weather Guide Service, an outfit teamed-up with nearby Anglers' Bay (a traditional, year-round fishing camp featuring lodging, bait, tackle, tips, and rentals of everything from clams and ATVs to power augers), learned that the most pleasant way possible: by catching, lots of them.

And he does it one rod at a time.

"Hell, I don't even own a tip-up," he confesses.

His secret: Concentration.

"Once I dig a hole, it becomes a cosmic vacuum. Everything I have ends up in it," he admits.

Craig Storms and Ice "Eye."

"On second thought," he interjects, taking his eyes off the screen for a split second, "I should have said two holes. I need one for my MarCum LX5 sonar."

Storms is well on his way to middle age. But he was a youngster when the digital world jumped the tracks from strictly military stuff to civilian recreational purposes. He uses all the contemporary gadgets to pursue fish: a GPS app on his smartphone to get him to the bar, electric power auger, and, most importantly, the sonar.

"It's an adult video game," he boasts. The favorite bait of the former Merchant Marine's (he served on ships bringing supplies to our troops during Desert Storm) is a Slender Spoon. He tips the hardware with the upper half of a pinched buckeye.

He actually lets his left thumbnail grow all winter long just so he can pinch minnows. "My wife is always asking me to cut the thing," he says, showing it off.

Storms uses a Navionics GPS Map Chip to turn his smart phone into a guiding light. It not only gets him to the bar's drop-off, it shows him where the inside bends, his favorite structures, are located. He starts by drilling a couple of holes in 20 feet of water, and moves to as deep as the mid 30-foot level looking for active fish.

Dropping his offering to bottom, he lifts it a few inches off the floor and goes to work forcefully jigging the lure, 4 to 6 inches, several times in rapid succession, punctuated by an arm-long sweep. When he sees a line (on the graph, fish appear as short horizontal lines) start following his bait, he slows his pace and steadily lifts the offering, always keeping the lure moving slowly, temptingly above the walleye.

"Seeing a line separating from bottom and head for your lure is very exciting. When the graph shows it merging with the bait, the temptation to set the hook can be overwhelming. But don't do it!" he advises. . "Wait until you feel the hit before setting the hook."

Watching this angler ice-fishing you can't help but notice how much he gives to the lake. But he claims to receive more than he dishes out.

"For instance, Spider," he says, launching a dreamy expression over his face, "hearing the lake's prenatal symphony of groans while it makes ice; feeling a surprise icequake shake the whole shanty as the ice cracks or throws a ridge, sometimes underneath you; the thrill of a walleye darting in and out of view in the 8-inch hole . . . These things are priceless," he explains.

"After catching a limit of 'eyes,' I go for a limit of perch; what we call an Oneida Lake Grand slam. It happens rarely, only about 1 time out of 25, but when it does, you know you've had a really good day," he says, with amazing understatement.

"They hang out in the same places and respond to the same bait and techniques the walleye do. The only big difference is they tend to be a little shallower. I look for them by drilling a couple of holes at the bends, in 18 to 22 feet of water, and keep moving until I find a school of hungry ones," he explains.

Another nice thing about the Vienna Bar is the lake's high, northeastern bank. When the notoriously severe north wind slams into it, the landmass blocks the shot, deflecting it out into the lake. In many years, the spot is one of the first to develop safe ice.

The state's Jewell ice-fishing parking area on Wanner Road (off NY 49, a couple of miles west of North Bay), offers two plowed lots with enough room for about 50 cars. Follow the trail off the southeastern corner of the lower lot to the water.

60. DRILLING FOR "EYES" OFF LEWIS POINT

Oneida Lake's eastern basin is wide and relatively featureless, pretty boring from a walleye's point of view. Fishing it in warm weather is relatively easy because all you have to do is throw a couple of jigs tipped with worm halves, or whole crawlers on harnesses, plain or spinner-rigged, over the side and drift around. Sooner or later you're going to run into a hungry fish.

Winter's a different story; ice stops drifting cold. But don't tell that to cousin Staash (he just got a MarCum ShowDown Ice-troller Digital FishFinder and it went to his head). He'll argue with you, claiming he does it all the time: "I drill 10 to 15 holes, set tip-ups in five, and go from one hole to the other working spikes on ice jigs, or hardware tipped with buckeyes gently on bottom. I call it ice drifting," he adds. Staash's strategy is a popular one. But instead of running around all over the lake sounding bottom with fish detectors, most guys targeting walleye through the ice concentrate on areas offering deep structure. And, gallon for gallon, the spot with the greatest collection of structure on the extreme eastern end of the lake, all within a few hundred feet of the bank, is Lewis Point.

Burt Menninger, a south shore resident who's been fishing the point for over 50 years, surmises the reason walleyes are especially attracted to the spot is because of its steep, rocky, inshore drop-off, and its close proximity to ideal winter walleye habitat like Messenger Reef (a mile due west), and Messenger Shoal and the pancakes surrounding it (a mile northwest).

Menninger fishes in water ranging from 15 to 18 feet deep. "I'll set a line of tip-ups baited with large buckeyes—3-inchers if I can get 'em—or fatheads, then sit on a bucket and jig a minnow on a Swedish Pimple or other hardware."

"If perch are around, I'll tip the hardware with a perch eye or spike. Perch eyes used to be very popular in the last century. But they fell out of favor for some reason. Now they're coming back," he adds.

"Another popular bait around here is a Heddon Sonar," Menninger continues. "It's all a lot of guys use. Just vertically jig it a couple of inches off bottom."

"In fact," he says, after a moment's thought, "a Sonar makes a great fish caller. Dig an extra hole near your tip-ups and snap-jig it. The vibration will draw fish from all around."

As mentioned earlier, Lewis Point is owned by McCraith Beverages, Inc., a firm out of New York Mills, and is closed from April 1 through Oct 15. Public fishing is permitted the rest of the time. A parking lot big enough for 20 or more cars is on the right side, at the end of Lewis Point Road. Follow the signs to the water.

61. PERCH IN THE MUD OFF CHAPMAN PARK

This Town of Sullivan property is another of the lake's ice-fishing hot spots. Perch are drawn to the area by its soft bottom. Anglers are drawn by the perch and the park's large, plowed parking lot and easy access to the water.

Fishing Camp.

"Mud pretty much covers the floor clear across the lake," says Burt Menninger, a local railroad retiree who has lived in Lakeport, a stone's throw from the water, for over 50 years. "Perch feed on the scuds and mud worms that thrive in the stuff."

"This is one of the lake's best ice-fishing spots for perch," claims Menninger, adding "especially during early ice."

He suggests fishing mousies a couple of inches off bottom, in 25 to 30 feet of water. Use a tiny bobber, and enough split shot to get the bait down.

According to Menninger, an old Oneida Lake technique is still practiced around here. It involves placing a tiny bobber 4 or 5 inches above the bait, and enough split shot between them to take the whole rig to bottom.

"Let out only enough line to get to bottom," advises Burt. "Keep an eye on the bobber as it goes down. If you see it stop before it reaches the end of the line, set the hook because a perch has it."

"But I'll tell ya," he warns, "you fish for a whole day like that and you'll be exhausted by evening."

Although not as plentiful as they are at Lewis Point, walleyes are known to come around, especially along the steep drop-off north of Blind Isle (the shallowest point on Lakeport Shoal). They're normally taken by guys targeting perch with buckeyes or flatheads off tip-ups, vertically jigged bladebaits, and shiny hardware tipped with minnows.

Ron Gasowski, aka the "Tip-up King," suggests fishing in 18 to 20 feet of water with a tungsten teardrop jig tipped with a fathead minnow. "Tungsten's characteristics get it to bottom quicker than jigs made of other heavy metals," he claims, adding "and it draws perch better, too."

Gasowski has another claim to fame that earns him the admiration of leisure-minded anglers everywhere: fishing from late morning through late afternoon. "I'd go earlier," says the middle-aged King, "but I prefer 10 to 4 because that's the warmest part of the day."

The park is located on NY 31, about a mile west of Lakeport.

62. BILLINGTON: BURT'S BAY

Having lived within casting distance of the water for almost 60 years, Burt Menninger knows a lot about Oneida Lake; so much, in fact, that in the last century a lot of folks along the south shore used him as a barometer in determining the state of the lake's fishery. It was common to walk into a bait shop, restaurant, even gas station and hear "If Burt ain't catching 'em, nobody is." (Some locals argue there's a lot of Burts on the lake.)

Age has slowed him down a little but it hasn't stopped him. Nowadays, you won't find him waist-deep in the rapids of Caughdenoy, vying for a choice spot on the walls in Sylvan Beach, or even among the crowd wading out into the autumn surf in front of his house. He's exchanged the fast-paced excitement of fishing with the crowd for quiet moments on the water with good friends. When winter casts its squeaky-clean pall over the landscape, creating his favorite fishing conditions, Burt heads for the relatively obscure, peaceful ice on Billington Bay.

His main draw is perch. Typically ranging from a solid 8 to 13 inches—some even better—they're drawn here by a wide shelf, running in a diagonal line between Damon and Shackelton Points, that slips gently from 14 to 30 feet of water. Sounding bottom the old way, by using a heavy weight on the line, he searches for their preferred depth of 18 to 20 feet.

Finding a spot that feels good (he doesn't use a fish finder . . . or cell phone, for that matter), he drills a few holes, tips his hardware with a perch eye or minnow (he prefers buckeyes but says fatheads work just as well) and drops it straight down. When it reaches bottom, he raises the offering a few inches off the floor and jigs.

"Perch eyes used to be very popular back in the day, but fell out of favor for a while" he says. "Now they're coming back," he reports with a beaming smile.

Billington Bay is lined with private property. According to most of the people who fish it, many other spots that are just as good are easier to reach. Still, if you like the thought of elbow room and silence while ice-fishing, you

Cazenovia, NY, resident Hunter Sattler's Bucket Running Over.

can reach the place by parking in the NYSDEC's South Shore Fishing Access site, and heading west for about a mile, to the magic depths on the other side of Shackleton Point.

63. CLEVELAND'S LAWYERS

Burbot are Oneida Lake's most misunderstood native fish. Slimy, looking like a cross between a catfish and an eel, these bottom dwellers are called a litany of nasty names like lawyer and snakehead, and are treated with prejudice by intellectually challenged anglers. They used to be so common up until early in the last century, anglers built ice shelters out of them ("Ecology and Economics of Oneida Lake Fish," Bulletin of the New York State College of Forestry at Syracuse University, Adams and Hankinson, 1928).

The year's first fish to spawn, and the only species to do it under the ice, they come out of the depths "in throbbing masses, like balls of rattlesnakes," says Randy Jackson, Senior Research Associate at Cornell's Biological Field Station, and release their milt and eggs into the sediment-choked waters they roil.

Requiring deep, clean habitat, they're out of the range of anglers for most of the year. Come winter, consistent temperatures throughout the water column, and their urge to spawn, increase their range . . . and their chances of running into a baited hook. Unfortunately, their rare encounter with humans usually finds them tossed on the ice to die and feed the seagulls.

That's a shame because they're very good eating; a prized delicacy in Northern Europe, and in states with large populations of Scandinavian descendants. In fact, an international Eelpout (another name for the species) Festival is held each February in the hamlet of Walker, Minnesota (population 1069 in 2013), on Leech Lake, to celebrate one of the world's "ugliest bottom-dwelling fish."

But if you want to catch one of these homely critters, you better hurry. "Although they're still relatively common, their numbers are declining, probably because of warming water temperatures. If the warming trend continues at the rate it's going, they'll probably disappear from the lake in the next 50 to 90 years," predicts Jackson.

The waters off the hamlet of Cleveland host more than their fair share of lawyers. Guys who ice-fish for yellow perch and walleye on the drop-off along the bar named after the hamlet catch them all the time, sometimes two or three a day.

A lot of the anglers who stop into Apps Landing (a popular bait shop tucked into the corner of Cleveland Dock Fishing Access Site), after a day on the ice to warm up and gather intelligence from the old timers who often hang out there, claim many of their lawyers hit just below the ice, something you don't expect from a bottom dweller.

Jackson offers this explanation: "Burbot are very adept predators, and will feed on just about anything that moves. It's likely they'll follow a minnow, striking it just below the ice. Others are probably taken in shallow water while spawning."

The area's main attractions for lawyers seem to be Cleveland Bar's steep drop-off into the lake's deepest water; and the mouth of Black Creek, a tributary that runs into Wells Bay's northwestern corner, Apps Landing.

64. TAFT BAY

This bay's relatively gentle slope takes about 0.5 mile to drop to 20 feet, so it's not favored by walkers. But don't let its lack of obvious structure discourage you. Its proximity to Taft Point, where bottom takes a steep dive into deep water, makes this a popular launch site for mechanized icers targeting perch and walleye, especially later in the season when walleye converge on the area in preparation for their spawning run up Scriba Creek.

The town of Constantia's David C. Webb Memorial Park is always plowed and offers parking for about 30 cars with trailers. It's located on NY 49, 2.7 miles east of the Oneida Lake Hatchery at Constantia.

The DEC offers an ice-fishing access site about 500 yards west of the park, just beyond the first house. It isn't used very often because the trek through the woods is arduous and the lot isn't always plowed.

65. HITCHCOCK POINT

Maple Bay Bar, a shallow shelf built out of sediments deposited over the millennia by Chittenango Creek, reaches due north from Hitchcock Point. Several hundred yards out, it splits, sending Crans Bar west and Northwest Bar north. Eel Isle, a shallow shoal, rises out of the east side of Northwest Bar.

This collection of structure and depths makes the place a smallmouth hot spot in summer. Come winter, the drop-offs along the bars and the deep flats turn into yellow perch magnets. And late winter sees walleyes swarm into the area in preparation for their spawning run up Chittenango Creek, one of the lake's main pike nurseries. Their bite improves steadily the closer you get to their season's close.

Fisher Bay Restaurant (315-633-2244), the classiest eatery in Bridgeport, and one of the finest on the lake, is about 0.5 mile east of the point. The owners have a long history on Oneida Lake and allow the public access from their property, and even allow parking in their lot. Mary, one of the managers, says there's only one requirement: that you come into the restaurant to let her know who you are and to get instructions on where to park.

Lorne Rudy, the owners' son, adds: "Come autumn, the surf bite for walleye is dynamite right in front of the restaurant."

From the NY 31 traffic light on the east side of Chittenango Creek in Bridgeport, head up North Road for about a mile and turn left on Barrett Lane. The restaurant is at the end of the road.

66. CONSTANTIA ON ICE

Close proximity (less than 0.25 mile) to a drop descending to depths of over 16 feet makes this spot hugely popular with ice fishermen. Roving schools of yellow perch gravitate towards the near-shore drop.

Due south of the village center, a deep channel runs between Grassy and Little Islands and the Wantry Pyramid. Walleyes start coming around as early as January. Their numbers grow steadily as the season winds down and they stage off Scriba Creek in preparation for spawning.

The access site on Mill Street, a couple of blocks west of the Oneida Lake Fish Culture Station, offers parking for about 15 cars. This is a popular launch for car-top craft in summer.

Cool date: A couple's reward.

67. VERONA BEACH STATE PARK

Although the water is very shallow for about the first hundred yards or so, it drops to 20 feet deep less than 0.25 mile from shore. Roving walleye, yellow perch and white perch like to cruise the drop-off and are popularly targeted by ice anglers jigging hardware tipped with clipped buckeyes. They're not always there, but if you get lucky, the action never ends.

The huge lot is always plowed, and no day use fee is charged in winter.

The park is located on NY 13, about a mile south of Sylvan Beach.

APPENDIX

FISHING GUIDES AND CHARTER SERVICES

Ray Brown's Fishing Charters
604 Auburn Heights
Auburn, NY 13021
315-439-7236

Capt. Tony Buffa's Fishing Charters
9037 Lucas Road
Bridgeport, NY 13030
315-427-2278

Todd Frank
4081 Port Street
Pulaski, NY 13142
315-778-1598

McGrath & Associates Carp Angling Services
315-314-7154
315-882-1549
mmcgrath2@twcny.rr.com

Capt. Rick Miick
Dream Catcher Charters and Guide Service
247 Hadley Road
Sandy Creek, NY 13145
315-387-5920
www.trophydreamcatcher.com

Pat Miura
1417 State Street
Watertown, NY 13601
315-777-3570
pmiura@aol.com

Scriba Fishing Charters
135 CR 65
Bernhards Bay, NY 13028
315-380-6484

Stormy Weather Guide Service
607-316-7185
Craig.storms@gmail.com

BAIT AND TACKLE

Anglers' Bay
812 State Route 49
Cleveland, NY 13042
315-675-3662
www.fishoneida.com

Apps Landing
Lake Street (NY 49)
Cleveland, NY 13042
315-675-8334
According to owner Rick Sorensen: "We're open pretty steady
in May and June; every day during safe ice."

Bartel Road Bait & Tackle
5501 Bartel Road, Ste. 12
Brewerton, NY 13029
315-676-2144
BRBT@windstream.net

Bouf's Bait and Tackle
6830 Main Street
Verona Beach, NY 13162
315-877-2499
boufsbaitandtackle@yahoo.com

Caughdenoy Marina
10316 Caughdenoy Road
Central Square, NY 13036
315-668-8146

Charley's Boat Livery
82 McCloud Road
West Monroe, NY 13167
315-668-6341
www.OneidaLakeFishing.com

Cookie's Bait & Tackle
7627-Rt 298
Kirkville, NY 13082
315-633-5378

Gander Mountain
5864 Carmenica Drive
Cicero, NY 13039
315-698-1100

i 1 Baits
Mike Yarema
281 CR 12
Phoenix, NY 13135
315-575-1743
www.i1baits.com

Kirch's Three Pines Marina
2050-2054 Lake Shore Drive North
Blossvale, NY 13308
315-264-4198

Marion Manor Marina
NY 13
Canastota, NY 13032
315-762-4810
www.Marionmanor.com

Mickey's Live Bait & Tackle Shop
715 South Bay Road
North Syracuse, NY 13212
315-458-7998
www.fishingcny.com

South Shore Nautical, LLC
3728 State Route 31
Canastota, NY 13032
315-391-9213
www.southshorenautical.com

MARINAS

A&P Marina
7512 Murry Drive West
Cicero, NY 13039
315-699-7732

Aero Marina
9080 Beach Road
Brewerton, NY 13029
315-699-7736
www.aeromarina.com

Bay Marina
155 Camic Road
Central Square, NY 13036-3108
315-676-2223

Boathouse Marina, Bar and Restaurant
1397 NYS Rte. 49
Constantia, NY 13044

Callahan's Marina, Inc.
9089 Callahan Drive
Canastota, NY 13032
315-697-7470

Fisher Bay Boats and Marina
302 Barrett Road
Bridgeport, NY 13030
315-633-9657

Fremac Marine
1801 Route 31
Bridgeport, NY 13030
315-633-2661

Johnnies Pier 31
3653 State Highway 31
Canastota, NY 13032
315-697-7007

Johnson Bay Marina
150 McCloud Road
West Monroe, NY 13167
315-668-3453

Mariners Landing
705 Pioneer Avenue
Sylvan Beach, NY 13157
315-762-0112

Oneida Lake Marina LLC
3713 State Route 31
Canastota, NY 13032
315-697-4867

Pirates Cove Marina
9170 Horseshoe Island Road
Clay, NY 13041
315-695-3901
www.piratescovemarina.com

Snug Harbor Resort
1515 Willow Drive
Verona Beach, NY
315-762-5104

Spruce Grove Marina
1193 State Route 49
Constantia, NY 13044
315-623-9436
www.sprucegrovemarina.biz

Trade-A-Yacht East
613 CR 37
Brewerton, NY 13029
315-676-3531

PARKS

Joseph F. Williams Memorial Park
Town of Cicero Parks
8236 Brewerton Road
Cicero, NY 13039
315-699-5233

Oneida Shores Park
9400 Bartel Road
Brewerton, NY 13029
315-676-7366

Vernoa Beach State Park
Box 245 Route 13
Verona Beach, NY 13162
315-762-4463
For reservations, go to www.reserveamerica.com
or call 1-800-456-2267
Lock 23
315-676-4171

COUNTY TOURISM OFFICES

While the tourism offices listed below offer information on a wealth of attractions the whole family can enjoy, Oswego County Tourism's "Fishing and Hunting" guide contains the most complete information on fishing Oneida Lake.

Madison County Tourism
PO Box 1029
Morrisville, NY 13408
315-684-7320

Oneida County Tourism
PO Box 551
Utica, NY 13505
888-999-6560

Onondaga County
Syracuse Convention Visitor's Bureau
572 South Salina Street
Syracuse, NY 13202
800-234-4797
www.visitsyracuse.org

Oswego County Tourism
46 East Bridge Street
Oswego, NY 13126
315-349-8324
www.visitoswegocounty.com
www.fishingandhuntinginoswego.blogspot.com/

CHAMBERS OF COMMERCE

Fort Brewerton/Greater Oneida Lake Chamber of Commerce
315-668-3408
info@oneidalakechamber.com

OTHER CONTACTS

Village of Sylvan Beach
POB 508
Sylvan Beach, NY 13157
315-762-4844
www.sylvanbeach.org

INDEX